All I Ever Wanted to Know about Donald Trump I Learned From His Tweets

@realDonaldTrump

All I Ever Wanted to Know about Donald Trump I Learned From His Tweets
@realDonaldTrump

A Psychological Exploration of the President via Twitter

Compiled and edited by
Rachel Montgomery

Introduction by
John Gartner, PhD

Skyhorse Publishing

Skyhorse Publishing books may be purchased in bulk at special discounts for sales promotion, corporate gifts, fund-raising, or educational purposes. Special editions can also be created to specifications. For details, contact the Special Sales Department, Skyhorse Publishing, 307 West 36th Street, 11th Floor, New York, NY 10018 or info@skyhorsepublishing.com.

Skyhorse® and Skyhorse Publishing® are registered trademarks of Skyhorse Publishing, Inc.®, a Delaware corporation.

Visit our website at www.skyhorsepublishing.com.

10 9 8 7 6 5 4 3 2 1

Library of Congress Cataloging-in-Publication Data is available on file.

Cover design by Rain Saukas

Print ISBN: 978-1-5107-2983-4
Ebook ISBN: 978-1-5107-2984-1

Printed in the United States of America

Table of Contents

Should Trump Run?
(His Early Tweets)

America needs a President who can negotiate better deals for the American People.

AUG 25, 2011 2:49 PM

The people at shouldtrumprun.com have got it right! How are our factories supposed to compete with China and other countries...

JAN 27, 2011 4:13 PM

...when they have no environmental restrictions! America' s workers need us." http://shouldtrumprun.com/

JAN 27, 2011 4:14 PM

To this day, I don't know if Donald Trump ran on his own.

He did, literally. But what I'm specifically asking is whose bright idea was it that he run? His own? Or people that made it seem like he came up with the idea and he ran with it?

I had the privilege of speaking with Michael Cohen from *The Boston Globe* after a panel discussion on covering our forty-fifth president and his tweets. The discussion was about how journalists can effectively cover Trump. The key is to call out his bad behavior without sensationalizing it. However, how do you call out blown-up behavior without sounding over-the-top? Cohen was once cautioned by his editor for calling Trump a liar when he had clearly lied. Multiple times.

And when the POTUS is exhibiting behavior that looks like a personality disorder—how do you call that out? Can you? Should you?

I'm not a psychologist. I cannot and will not make an armchair diagnosis of Trump based on his tweets alone. I will say based on many of his statements that he is a liar, and I will go so far as to say he is a con artist. He is using his publicity and the presidency to stir up old prejudices and divides, and to see how far he can go with making policies that divide families and strip away liberties. He does all this in the name of "law and order" so that his base, rural and middle America, can sleep at night.

Like the businessman he is, he is drudging up our most prominent prejudices and using them to gather support. The xenophobia he's drudging up did not exist in a vacuum. September 11, 2001 heightened Islamophobia in our country. Anti-immigrant sentiment is as old as America itself. The human faces that our current time slaps on that hate are Mexican and Latin American; they used to be German, Irish, Italian, Polish, and Chinese.

The framework that Trump is working with was there long before him and long before Twitter. The groundwork was laid by Republicans and Democrats alike. The 1994 Crime Bill propelled mass incarceration. The Patriot Act suspended habeas corpus, allowed mass surveillance, and yes, Barack Obama deported more undocumented immigrants than George W. Bush. Trump's predecessors gave him the groundwork, but he is attempting to finish the job by communicating with the public via Twitter.

So what do his tweets do? Not all of them will sound insane without context. A good chunk of his political tweets frame the US as a declining, weak nation that needs a strong leader (like him) to face our many enemies (inside and out, real, imagined, or distorted). Our time is so limited now that we remember soundbites more than we do books or articles that can explain context and nuance. Trump uses Twitter to get these soundbites out there, and repeats them often using a core set of buzzwords to create a narrative that he is the savior our country needs, because middle America's fears (blasted at them from certain media outlets and corners of the Internet) of "The Other" are 100 percent real. Trump takes his fan base seriously to fan the flames and keep America divided while he consolidates as much power as he can.

What we can do to stop him or slow him down will be debated over the next four years. The independent investigation into possible Trump campaign collusion with Russia's tampering in our election may pan out. It may not. Trump could decide being president is too hard and resign with a 4 a.m. tweet. The future is uncertain. But one thing is true: other presidents have lied, spied, and behaved in a demagogue fashion, but it has never been with the intensity and speed this man is showing. I felt before reading his tweets that we were in uncharted waters with this administration, and while I know we've seen some of his behaviors before, his tweets have strengthened my belief that our democracy and society will never be the same. We live in a post-President Trump world now.

Everything You Ever Wanted to Know about Donald Trump's Mental Illness You Can Learn from His Tweets

By John Gartner, PhD

One of the most notable things about the 34,000 tweets that the author culled through to write this book is their sheer quantity. It's like looking at your phone in the morning, the night after a brief dinner date, and finding thirty-seven nasty texts from your date. The quantity alone warns that this person may not be mentally stable, and then the gratuitous nastiness confirms it. Donald Trump's manic dark energy drives him to vaunt himself and denigrate his fellow human beings relentlessly: all day, all night, every day, and every night.

To make sense of his aberrant behavior, you need to understand, specifically, what is psychologically wrong with Donald Trump. His diagnosis is the Rosetta Stone to cracking the Trump Twitter code, revealing its underlying structure, and unfortunately, how much danger all the rest of us are in as a result. He is a malignant narcissist who is also on the bipolar spectrum. From a psychiatric perspective, the prognosis could not be more dire—for us.

Much has been written about Trump having Narcissistic Personality Disorder. For example, Trump embodies the diagnostic criteria of believing himself to be "uniquely superior," ("Only *I* can fix it") to a degree that would be comical if it weren't so frightening. He appears to literally believe that he knows more about everything than everybody, despite his lack of experience, study, intellectual curiosity, or even normal attention span. An amusing video montage made its way through social media, where through the miracle of editing, in the course of three minutes Trump brags about being the world's greatest expert in twenty different subject areas, literally using the exact same sentence—just fill in the blank. "No one knows more about (fill in the blank) than me," he repeats over and over, while it becomes more absurd, as his imagined portfolio of expertise expands with each improbable bombastic claim. When candidate Trump was asked from whom he sought foreign policy advice, he responded, "I'm speaking with myself, number one, because I have a very good brain." Just how good a brain he has is up for debate, but the narcissistic fantasy that any brain is *so* good it doesn't need a brain trust bigger than me, myself, and I, is scary and crazy. "I know more about ISIS than the generals, believe me," he boasts. Trump has more ways to say, "I am the best" than anybody. Believe me.

But as critics have pointed out, merely saying a leader is narcissistic is hardly disqualifying. Most are. But *malignant narcissism* is to garden variety Narcissistic Personality Disorder what a malignant tumor is to a benign one. Both are bad, but only one will kill you.

"The quintessence of evil," was how Erich Fromm described malignant narcissism, a term he introduced in 1964.[1] Fromm, a refugee from Nazi Germany, developed the diagnosis to explain Adolf Hitler. While Fromm is most well-known as one of the founders of Humanistic Psychology—the basic premise of which is, ironically, that man's basic nature is good—the Holocaust survivor had a lifelong obsession with the psychology of evil. Malignant narcissism was, according to Fromm, "the most severe pathology. The root of the most vicious destructiveness and inhumanity."[2] Erich Fromm saw evil up close and applied his genius to boil it down to its psychological essence. A malignant narcissist is a human monster. He may not be as bad as Hitler, but according to Fromm he is cut from the same cloth: "The Egyptian Pharaohs, the Roman Caesars, the Borgias, Hitler, Stalin, Trujillo— they all show certain similar features."[3]

My former teacher Otto Kernberg is the modern figure most associated with the study of malignant narcissism. He defined the syndrome as having four components: 1) Narcissistic Personality Disorder, 2) antisocial behavior, 3) paranoid traits, and 4) sadism. [4] Kernberg told the *New York Times* that malignantly narcissistic leaders like Hitler or Stalin are "able to take control because their inordinate narcissism is expressed in grandiosity, a confidence in themselves and the assurance that they know what the world needs."[5] At the same time, "they express their aggression in cruel and sadistic behavior against their enemies: whoever does not submit to them or love them."[6]

As G. H. Pollock wrote, "the malignant narcissist is pathologically grandiose, lacking in conscience and behavioral regulation with characteristic demonstrations of joyful cruelty and sadism."[7]

When you combine these four ingredients—narcissism, antisocial traits, paranoia, and sadism—you have a leader who feels omnipotent, omniscient, and entitled to total power, who rages at being persecuted by imaginary enemies, which includes anyone who disagrees with him, as well as vulnerable minority groups who represent no threat whatsoever. All who are not part of the in-group or those who do not kiss his ring must be destroyed. And destroying them in the most humiliating and painful way will be an exquisite pleasure. Once you understand the logic of malignant narcissism, all of Trump's tweets make perfect sense.

Paranoia

In the same week, the *New York Times* and the *Washington Post* both ran front-page stories about Trump as a conspiracy theorist. Before the election, Rightwing Watch accumulated a list of fifty-eight conspiracies proclaimed by Trump. And of course, the list has grown since then. Many are truly bizarre. For example, not only is Barack Obama a

Muslim born in Kenya, but according to Trump, Obama had a Hawaiian government bureaucrat murdered to cover up the truth about his birth certificate:

> How amazing, the State Health Director who verified copies of Obama's "birth certificate" died in plane crash today. All others lived
>
> DEC 12, 2013 04:32:44 PM

Antonin Scalia was murdered: "They say they found a pillow on his face, (which is a pretty unusual place to find a pillow.)"[8]

Later, fake news websites sponsored by the Russians laid this "murder" at Hillary Clinton's feet. Fellow candidate Ted Cruz's father even aided the Kennedy assassination—the mother of all conspiracy theories. "What was he doing with Lee Harvey Oswald shortly before the death? Before the shooting? It's horrible."[9]

Yet, the world was shocked when Trump accused Barack Obama by tweet of illegally wiretapping Trump Tower. Why were we surprised when this tweeting about conspiracy theories has been going on for years, as the author's research shows?

Antisocial Personality Disorder

Trump also meets criteria for Antisocial Personality Disorder. Antisocials lie, exploit, and violate the rights of others, and have neither remorse nor empathy for those they harm.

Politifact estimated 76 percent of Trump's statements were false or mostly false, and *Politico* estimated Trump told a lie every three minutes and fifteen seconds.[10] So in his tweets, Trump freely and frequently lies. He doubles, triples, quadruples, and quintuples down on transparently disprovable falsehoods.

We have ample evidence of Trump's pervasive pattern of exploiting and violating the rights of others. According to New York Attorney General Eric Schneiderman, Trump University was a "straight up fraud…a fraud from beginning to end."[11] Dozens of lawsuits attest to his pattern and practice of not paying his contractors. Finally, there is Trump's pattern of serial sexual assault, which he bragged about on tape, even before a dozen women came forward, who he then called liars.

Trump is allergic to apology and appears to feel no remorse of any kind. It is as if being Trump means never having to say you're sorry. When Frank Luntz asked Trump if he had ever asked God for forgiveness, Trump said "I'm not sure I have...I don't think so."[12] His unrepentance notwithstanding, he also boasted that he loves God and his church.[13]

Sadism

Because he is a sadist, the malignant narcissist will take a bully's glee in persecuting, terrorizing, and even exterminating his "enemies" and scapegoats. When a protester was escorted out of a Trump rally, Trump famously said "I'd like to punch him in the face," in a tone that suggested it would genuinely bring him great pleasure.[14] He relished the thought of throwing another protester out in the cold without his coat. "I love the old days. You know what they used to do to guys like that when they were in a place like this? They'd be carried out on a stretcher, folks." Narcissists often hurt others in the pursuit of their selfish interests. A noteworthy difference between the normal Narcissistic Personality Disorder and the malignant narcissist is sadism, or the gratuitous enjoyment of the pain of others. A narcissist will purposely hurt other people in pursuit of their own desires, but may regret and, in some circumstances, show remorse for doing so, while a malignant narcissist will damage others and enjoy doing so, showing little compassion or shame for the damage they cause. People with simple Narcissistic Personality Disorder often feel shame when being forced to confront the reality that they have hurt other people in pursuit of their selfish or self-centered goals. For malignant narcissists it's a bonus. It's part of the fun.

Trump loves to "punch down" people that he views as weaker than himself by demeaning and humiliating them. Not only are sizable portions of Trump's 34,000 tweets dedicated to cyber-bullying, but sometimes, he will send the same nasty tweet six times across a day's news cycle day to maximize his victim's humiliation.

Trump lives in a paranoid zero sum world divided into two types of people: Winners and Losers. Strong and Weak. Victors and Vanquished. Bullies and Victims. Predator and Prey. The guys who get to grab the pussies and those that get their pussies grabbed. All that matters is coming out on top.

Winning Takes Care of Everything

As the author points out in her illuminating chapter "They Are Laughing at Us!" the worst thing Trump can say is *they* are winning. *They* are taking advantage. *They* are laughing at us. We should strike back at those bastards. Turn the tables, make them pay, and laugh in their faces.

> Lets fight like hell and stop this great and disgusting injustice! The world is laughing at us.
>
> Nov 6, 2012 8:30 PM

> The United States better address China's exchange rate before they steal our country and it is too late! China is laughing at us.
>
> Feb 25, 2013 6:54 PM

> "The Chinese laugh at how weak and pathetic our government is in combating intellectual property theft." (cont) http://tl.gd/g70qiu
>
> Mar 1, 2012 12:28 PM

Like the myth that the Inuit have one hundred words for snow, Trump has one hundred phrases to express his contempt (and that's *not* a myth). The quantity and tone of these insults say more about the insulter than about the people he is publicly verbally abusing. Here is a sample of some of the phrases used throughout his tweets: low life!, overrated, 3rd rate, lightweight incompetent clown, major sleaze and buffoon, total dud!, mental basket case, true garbage.

Trump's put-downs break into two basic categories: bad and weak. Losers are weak, and haters are bad. Indeed, haters and losers are his shorthand for anyone not on the Trump train:

> Happy Thanksgiving to all--even the haters and losers!
>
> Nov 27, 2013 2:22 PM

Happy Veterans Day to ALL, in particular to the haters and losers who have no idea how lucky they are!!!

Nov 11, 2013 7:59 AM

To EVERYONE, including all haters and losers, HAPPY NEW YEAR. Work hard, be smart and always remember, WINNING TAKES CARE OF EVERYTHING!

Dec 31, 2014 4:15 PM

The narcissist in him imagines he is superior to everyone in every way, so he must constantly assert he is more powerful in every respect. During the campaign he effectively diminished his Republican rivals as weak, making him the winner of the primate alpha male competition in a simple contest of fitness, size, and strength.

Leightweight chocker Marco Rubio looks like a little boy on stage. Not presidential material!

Deleted after 1 hour at 11:17 AM on Feb 26

Low energy candidate @JebBush has wasted $80 million on his failed presidential campaign. Millions spent on me. He should go home and relax!

Jan 21, 2016 6:32 AM

He loves to call his critics stupid—essentially accusing them of mental weakness. As in:

Highly untalented Wash Post blogger, Jennifer Rubin, a real dummy, never writes fairly about me. Why does Wash Post have low IQ people?

Dec 1, 2015 12:46 PM

How many ways can Trump call someone stupid? Let us count the ways: dumb as a rock, truly dumb as a rock, dummy dope, total dope!, very, very dumb!, dumbest of them all, lowest IQ on television, a

xviii   All I Ever Wanted to Know about Donald Trump I Learned From His Tweets

spoiled brat without a properly functioning brain, gets dumber each &
every year--& started from a very low base.

> Sorry losers and haters, but my I.Q. is one of the highest -and you
> all know it! Please don't feel so stupid or insecure,it's not your fault
>
> MAY 8, 2013 9:37 PM

If his critic is a woman, he will always find a weakness in her appearance:

> There are many editorial writers that are good, some great, & some
> bad. But the least talented of all is frumpy Gail Collins of NYTimes.
>
> MAR 17, 2014 2:03 PM

> Frumpy and very dumb Gail Collins, an editorial writer at The
> New York Times, is so lucky to even have a job. Check her out
> - incompetent!
>
> MAR 15, 2014 4:31 PM

> Huffington Post is just upset that I said its purchase by AOL has
> been a disaster and that Arianna Huffington is ugly both inside
> and out!
>
> APR 20, 2014 4:57 PM

At his rallies, he said about one of the women who accused him of
sexual assault, "Believe me, she would not be my first choice, that I
can tell you," implying she wasn't attractive enough to assault.[15] When
asked about his rival Carly Fiorina, he said: "Look at that face! Would
anyone vote for that? Can you imagine that, the face of our next president?!"[16]

At the Republican debate Megyn Kelly confronted him with this
pattern: "You've called women you don't like fat pigs, dogs, slobs, and
disgusting animals."

"Only Rosie ODonnell," was his tone-deaf answer[17], illustrating
the very problem Kelly was talking about. But apparently he thought

his answer was hilarious:

> Rosie O'Donnell was the best answer of that whole debate
>
> AUG 7, 2015 4:05 AM

And then he turned the same treatment on Kelly:

> I refuse to call Megyn Kelly a bimbo, because that would not be politically correct. Instead I will only call her a lightweight reporter!
>
> JAN 27, 2016 3:44 AM

Because Trump is also paranoid. Those who stand in his way are not just weak (i.e., stupid, ugly losers), they are also all bad. Really bad. Liars, connivers, scum, maliciously trying to attack and destroy him because they are such haters. He is a victim of their malice—which is really a projection. No one is nastier than Donald Trump. He is a victimizer who feels like a victim.

> The failing @nytimes is truly one of the worst newspapers. They knowingly write lies and never even call to fact check. Really bad people!
>
> MAR 13, 2016 11:53 AM

> .@AP continues to do extremely dishonest reporting. Always looking for a hit to bring them back into relevancy—ain't working!
>
> NOV 23, 2015 8:22 AM

> .@politico has no power, but so dishonest!
>
> OCT 7, 2015 8:47 AM

> I was viciously attacked by Mr. Khan at the Democratic Convention. Am I not allowed to respond? Hillary voted for the Iraq war, not me!
>
> JUL 31, 2016 9:32 AM

To Trump all negative facts about him are lies. And all who tell them are liars who should be punished with the harsh treatment they deserve, which is why he has branded the *entire press,* "the enemy of the people."[18] It's not accidental that leaders like Stalin have used such phrases in an attempt to delegitimize a free press and justify a deadly purge. From Trump's language you would think, if only he had the power, he would do the same.

> Many journalists are honest and great - but some are knowingly dishonest and basic scum. They should.be weeded out!
>
> APR 6, 2015 11:42 PM

Because in the world of the malignant narcissist, those who you imagine are unfairly attacking you deserve the most severe retaliation.

> When someone attacks me, I always attack back...except 100x more. This has nothing to do with a tirade but rather, a way of life!
>
> NOV 11, 2012 8:56 AM

> When somebody challenges you unfairly, fight back - be brutal, be tough - don't take it. It is always important to WIN!
>
> JUN 27, 2015 10:50 AM

Though he can't actually kill reporters like his friend Vladimir Putin, Trump can kill them in fantasy, which is almost as good, because Trump believes his fantasies are real (like having the biggest crowd in history at his inauguration, for example). So the bad newspapers that are spreading lies about him are dying, and they deserve it. Trump has not executed them, instead their own weakness and badness is the cause of their death. But because of his sadism he takes immense pleasure in the suffering of his enemies and couldn't be more manically gleeful about their imagined demise. It never gets old rejoicing in the blood of your enemies.

> I was so happy when I heard that @Politico, one of the most dishonest political outlets, is losing a fortune. Pure scum!
>
> OCT 8, 2015 4:49 PM

> I love watching the dishonest writers @NYMag suffer the magazine's failure.
>
> OCT 18, 2013 11:27 AM

The reporting at the failing @nytimes gets worse and worse by the day. Fortunately, it is a dying newspaper.

AUG 19, 2016 5:43 AM

Sad thing is Rolling Stone was (is) a dead magazine with big downward circulation and now, for them at last, people are talking about it!

JUL 17, 2013 6:17 PM

National Review @NRO may be going out of business because of the really pathetic job being done by @JonahNRO. No talent means death - sad!

APR 20, 2015 7:12 PM

One of the country's dumbest newspapers—The Palm Beach Post-- should be put to sleep. It's dying. @pbpost

JAN 25, 2013 8:37 AM

In this next set of tweets, Trump simultaneously exults in the imaginary death of one his hometown newspapers, the *New York Daily News*, but still manages to compliment himself, because it's his photo that sells their newspapers:

.@NYDailyNews, the dying tabloid owned by dopey clown Mort Zuckerman, puts me on the cover daily because I sell. My honor, but it is dead!

JUN 28, 2015 4:23 PM

Like all narcissists he attributes the success of others to his own reflected glory:

Face The Nation's interview of me was the highest rated show that they have had in 15 years. Congratulations and WOW! @CBSNews @jdickerson

JAN 11, 2016 6:42 PM

.@ChuckTodd just informed us that my interview last week on @MeetthePress was their highest rated show in 4 years. Congrats!

OCT 6, 2015 11:46 AM

Just announced that in the history of @CNN, last night's debate was its highest rated ever. Will they send me flowers & a thank you note?

SEP 17, 2015 10:17 AM

There is no greeting card for this indirect form of self-congratulation. What would a card like that look like?

To my son on the day of his graduation. Congratulations on inheriting my fantastic DNA and having all the advantages my hard work has provided for you.

Love, Dad

At times, Trump's tweets reflect his glaring lack of basic human empathy—a hallmark of the psychopath. The most horrific human tragedies are, for Trump, merely opportunities to indulge his compulsive need to attack, denigrate, and boast:

If the morons who killed all of those people at Charlie Hebdo would have just waited, the magazine would have folded - no money, no success!

JAN 14, 2015 9:13 AM

Sorry to hear @msnbc was dead last, in the gutter, in their Boston bombing coverage http://bit.ly/15A4Msm @hardball_chris @Lawrence

APR 22, 2013 11:35 AM

After the Orlando massacre:

Appreciate the congrats for being right on radical Islamic terrorism, I don't want congrats, I want toughness & vigilance. We must be smart!

JUN 12, 2016 9:43 AM

But where we may really see Trump's antisocial side at work is in how he took advantage of, and may even have colluded with, the fake news and hacks perpetrated by the Russians to sway the election. At the time of this writing, new information pours in every day to support the unthinkable conclusion that our president may be the agent of a hostile foreign power with whom he allied to steal an election. If that proves true, Trump will be more than simply antisocial. He will go down in the all-time villain hall of fame, somewhere between Benedict Arnold and Judas.

Trump's Twitter account may be implicated in at least two respects. First, Russia flooded our social media with fake news, a technique they call "active measures." When asked by Senator James Lankford (R-OK) about why Russian President Vladimir Putin decided to make more of an effort to interfere in the 2016 presidential election than in years past, former FBI agent Clinton Watts said, "the answer is very simple and it's what nobody is really saying in this room…Part of the reason active measures have worked in this US election is because the Commander-in-Chief [Trump] has used Russian active measures at times, against his opponents."[19] Knowingly or unknowingly, Trump regularly retweeted Russian propaganda to his twenty-six million followers: "In some instances, Trump and his campaign team propagated fake stories they appear to have learned about directly from Russian state media."[20] So the whoops-I-didn't-know-it-was-Russian defense doesn't hold water. Trump used his Twitter account as a Russian propaganda laundromat.

The Russians were also fine-tuned in their understanding of Trump's Twitter habits. According to Watts, they "tweet at President Trump during high volumes when they know he's online and they push conspiracy theories." Watts provided an example: Trump "denies the intel from the United States about Russia. He claimed that the election could be rigged; that was the number one theme pushed by RT Sputnik news."[21]

Of course, in addition to active measures, the Russians hacked the DNC and released emails right before the Democratic convention, revealing internecine conflict within the party. Specifically, that party chairwoman Debbie Wasserman Schultz had favored Hillary Clinton, the establishment candidate. The dump was exquisitely timed to wreak maximum damage, to drive a spike between the Bernie and Hillary supporters, just as they needed to bury the hatchet and come together at the convention. Now that we know Trump's team may have had something to do with that dump, his exploitation of it seems even more dastardly.

The Wikileakes e-mail release today was so bad to Sanders that it will make it impossible for him to support her, unless he is a fraud!

DELETED AFTER 18 MINUTES AT 11:25 AM ON JUL 24,2016

I always said that Debbie Wasserman Schultz was overrated. The Dems Convention is cracking up and Bernieis exhausted, no energy left!

JUL 24, 2016 3:30 PM

Bernie should pull his endorsement of Crooked Hillary after she decieved him and then attacked him and his supporters.

OCT 2, 2016 4:48 PM

Crooked Hillary Clinton knew everything that her "servant" was doing at the DNC - they just got caught, that's all! They laughed at Bernie.

JUL 25, 2016 6:19 AM

How much BAD JUDGEMENT was on display by the people in DNC in writing those really dumb e-mails, using even religion, against Bernie!

JUL 25, 2016 6:57 AM

Bernie Sanders is being treated very badly by the Democrats - the system is rigged against him. Many of his disenfranchised fans are for me!

MAY 18, 2016 6:20 AM

Bernie Sanders is being treated very badly by the Dems. The system is rigged against him. He should run as an independent! Run Bernie, run.

MAY 16, 2016 5:00 AM

And Trump's denials that the Russians were involved, even when all seventeen of our intelligence agencies said that they were seems particularly suspicious:

The "Intelligence" briefing on so-called "Russian hacking" was delayed until Friday, perhaps more time needed to build a case. Very strange!

JAN 3, 2017 8:14 PM

Russia talk is FAKE NEWS put out by the Dems, and played up by the media, in order to mask the big election defeat and the illegal leaks

FEB 26, 2017 1:16 PM

Totally made up facts by sleazebag political operatives, both Democrats and Republicans - FAKE NEWS! Russiasays nothing exists. Probably...

JAN 13, 2017 6:11 AM

Russia just said the unverified report paid for by political opponents is "A COMPLETE AND TOTAL FABRICATION, UTTER NONSENSE." Very unfair!

JAN 11, 2017 7:13 AM

Julian Assange said "a 14 year old could have hacked Podesta" - why was DNC so careless? Also said Russians did not give him the info!

JAN 4, 2017 7:22 AM

But in contradiction to the idea that the Russians were not involved, Trump directly appealed to Russia to release Hillary's missing emails during the campaign. He said on national TV, "Russia, if you're listening, I hope you're able to find the 30,000 emails that are missing. I think you will probably be rewarded mightily by our press."[22] A similar sentiment he then echoed again on Twitter:

> If Russia or any other country or person has Hillary Clinton's 33,000 illegally deleted emails, perhaps they should share them with the FBI!
>
> JUL 27, 2016 11:16 AM

It's clear that Trump is one bad hombre, but one of the recurrent debates, and genuine mysteries, is to what extent is Trump just a really unscrupulous person and to what extent is he really divorced from reality?[23] Is Trump "crazy like a fox," or just crazy? It's often hard to know because, as Harvard psychoanalyst Lance Dodes put it, Trump tells two kinds of lies: The ones he tells others and those he tells himself: "He lies in the way anybody who scams people does. He's trying to sell an idea or a product by telling you something that's untrue. There's that lie. There's also the kind of lie he has that is in a way more serious. That he has a loose grip on reality."[24]

Before the election, I wrote in the *Huffington Post* a warning that Trump was a dangerous malignant narcissist. At that point, in June of 2016, there was still a strong hope that Trump would "pivot" and become more presidential—a slim hope based on a best-case scenario: Trump is a wicked con man, but still a rational actor, and thus he would pivot when it was in his own best interest. I wrote that "the idea that Trump is going to settle down and become presidential when he achieves power is wishful thinking. Success emboldens malignant narcissists to become even more grandiose, reckless and aggressive. Sure enough, after winning the nomination, there has been no 'pivot' towards more reasonable behavior and ideas, just the opposite. He has become more shrill, combative and openly racist."[25]

"Malignant narcissism is a madness that tends to grow in the life of the afflicted person," wrote Fromm.[26] They don't get better. They get worse.

After riding his angry base to the White House, to pivot to a saner presentation after the election would have been in Trump's best interest, to say the least. Many have wondered why Trump didn't just stop acting mentally ill. Because his illness is not a ruse, and can't just be turned off when it's convenient. In the *Huffington Post*, Michael J. Tansey, PhD wrote:Surpassing the devastation of climate, health care, education, diplomacy, social services, freedom of speech, liberty, and justice for all, nothing is more incomprehensible than the now-plausible prospect of all-out nuclear war…Because of this existential threat, it is absolutely urgent that we understand the differences between a president who is merely "crazy like a fox" (shrewd, calculating, the truth is only spoken when it happens to coincide with one's purposes) versus what I have termed "crazy like a crazy" (well-hidden core grandiose and paranoid delusions that are disconnected from reality).[27]

Insight into this question came from, of all sources, Joe Scarborough, host of the popular MSNBC show *Morning Joe*. Trump tweeted that Barack Obama had bugged Trump Tower:

> Terrible! Just found out that Obama had my "wires tapped" in Trump Tower just before the victory. Nothing found. This is McCarthyism!
>
> MAR 4, 2017 3:35 AM

Scarborough tweeted in response:

> His tweets this weekend suggest the president is not crazy like a fox. Just crazy.
>
> MAR 5, 2017 1:30 PM

Some of Trump's false claims can be seen as having a perverse strategic advantage for him. For example, his claim that Obama was not born in the United States appealed to the racist portion of the electorate who were already inclined to see a black president as foreign and illegitimate. But other false statements seem more blatantly crazy, precisely because they offer him no discernable strategic advantage.

Take his false claim that he had the biggest inaugural crowd in history. On the first day of his presidency, he lost credibility with the entire world with that demonstrably false claim (as Chico Marx, disguised as Groucho, said in *Duck Soup*, "who are you going to believe, me or your lying eyes?"), when there was no longer any need to motivate his base, which was already ecstatically celebrating his inauguration. At that point, he needed to broaden his base and shore up his authority as president, not pander to those he'd already won over. But he did the opposite.

For these same reasons, Michael Tansey argued that Trump meets Diagnostic and Statistical Manual of Mental Disorders Fifth edition criteria for Delusional Disorder, which simply requires evidence of a delusion lasting longer than a month in the absence of a more serious psychotic disorder such as schizophrenia or Bipolar 1 Disorder, which would in themselves explain the presence of delusional thinking.[28]

Trump isn't schizophrenic. That's one diagnosis we can definitively rule out. But we should explore where he fits on the bipolar spectrum. I believe Trump has the hypomanic temperament I wrote about in my two books, *The Hypomanic Edge: The Link Between (A Little) Craziness and (A Lot) of Success in America* and *In Search of Bill Clinton: A Psychological Biography*. Hypomanic temperament is genetically based, and runs in the families of people with bipolar relatives, but represents a milder and more functional expression of the same traits as mania. Historically, hypomanic temperament has received little attention compared to Bipolar Disorder, but the founders of modern psychiatry—Eugen Bleuler, Emil Kraepelin, Ernst Kretschmer—first described these personalities early in the twentieth century. In an article in the *New Republic*, I summarized the traits of hypomanic temperament as follows:

> Hypomanics are whirlwinds of activity who are filled with energy and need little sleep, less than 6 hours. They are restless, impatient and easily bored, needing constant stimulation and tend to dominate conversations. They are driven, ambitious and veritable forces of nature in pursuit of their goals. While these goals may appear grandiose to others, they are supremely confident of success—and no one can tell them otherwise. They can be

exuberant, charming, witty, gregarious but also arrogant. They are impulsive in ways that show poor judgment, saying things off the top of their head, and acting on ideas and desires quickly, seemingly oblivious to potentially damaging consequences. They are risk takers who seem oblivious to how risky their behavior truly is. They have large libidos and often act out sexually. Indeed all of their appetites are heightened.[29]

This description sounds an awful lot like Trump, who reports that he usually only sleeps four hours a night (and recommends others do the same in his 2004 book, *Think Like a Billionaire*), which by itself is a pretty reliable indicator of hypomania. He boasts about it in the book: "How can you compete against people like me if I sleep only four hours?"[30] He claims to work seven days a week, and in a typical eighteen-hour day make "over a hundred phone calls" and have "at least a dozen meetings."[31] "Without energy you have nothing!" tweeted Trump in 2015, hence his taunt of Jeb Bush as "a low energy person" by contrast, which proved quite effective.

Like most hypomanics, Trump is distractible. We could add Attention Deficit Disorder (ADD) to the Trump diagnostic list, except ADD almost always goes with the territory for most hypomanics. "Most successful people have very short attention spans. It has a lot to do with imagination," Trump wrote.[32] He is correct. The same rapidity of thought that helps engender creativity makes it difficult to stay on one linear track of ideas without skipping to the next. Like most hypomanics, Trump trusts his own ideas and judgment over any and everybody else, and follows his "vision, no matter how crazy or idiotic other people think it is."[33]

Of course, who sends 35,000 tweets and who tweets at three a.m.? Only a hypomanic. One of my dictums when working with hypomanic patients is that "nothing fails like success." If they succeed in achieving one of their wildly ambitious goals, there is often a noticeable uptick in their hypomania, sometimes even precipitating a full-blown hypomanic episode, which, unlike hypomanic temperament, is a diagnosable disorder. They become more aggressive, irritable, reckless, and impulsive. Now seemingly confirmed in their grandiosity, they drink their own Kool-Aid, and feel even more invincible and brilliant. They pursue even bolder, riskier, and more ambitious goals, without listening to dissent, doing their due diligence, or considering contradictory facts. Their gut is always right.

Once Trump was asked who he goes to for advice. With a straight face he said "myself." Trump is Trump's most trusted advisor. In the same vein, with the increase in grandiosity in a hypomanic, there is a corresponding increase in paranoia about the fools and rivals who might naysay their insights, impede their progress, or destroy them out of jealousy or ignorance.

In fact, this is a pattern for Trump. In 1988, after the publication of his bestselling *The Art of the Deal*, Trump's celebrity took off. His response was an increase in his hypomania, according to *Politico* writer Michael Kruse in his article, "1988: The Year Donald Lost his Mind." "It was the year Trump's insatiable appetites and boundless ego—this early, spectacular show of success—nearly did him in," Kruse wrote.[34]

He continued:

> His response to his surging celebrity was a series of manic, ill-advised ventures. He cheated on his wife, the mother of his first three children. In business, he was acquisitive to the point of recklessness. He bought and sold chunks of stocks of companies he talked about taking over. He glitzed up his gaudy yacht, the yacht the banks would seize less than three years later. He used hundreds of millions of dollars of borrowed money to pay high prices for a hotel and an airline—and his lenders would take them, too…his third casino in Atlantic City, the most expensive, gargantuan one yet, the Trump Taj Mahal, which led quickly to the first of his four corporate bankruptcy filings.[35]

Flash forward eighteen years to 2016, where Trump once again achieved success beyond anyone's wildest imagination. He became addicted to rallies where he excited crowds with his hypomanic charisma and they in turn threw gasoline on the fire of his hypomanic grandiosity, culminating in the Republican National Convention where he made the grandiose proclamation:

"Only I can fix it."

David Brooks is not a mental health professional but he astutely commented in August 2016 on what appeared to him to be Trump's increasing hypomania:

> He cannot be contained because he is psychologically off the chain. With each passing week he displays the classic symptoms of medium-grade mania in more disturbing forms: inflated self-esteem, sleeplessness, impulsivity, aggression and a compulsion to offer advice on subjects he knows nothing about. His speech patterns are like something straight out of a psychiatric textbook. Manics display something called "flight of ideas." It's a formal thought disorder in which ideas tumble forth through a disordered chain of associations. One word sparks another, which sparks another, and they're off to the races. As one trained psychiatrist said to me, compare Donald Trump's speaking patterns to a Robin Williams monologue, but with insults instead of jokes.[36]

But while Trump's 1988 hypomanic crash only resulted in a few bankruptcies, as president, the consequences could be on a scale too disturbing to contemplate.

When going through the following collection of Trump's tweets, one of the trends the reader should note is the progression over time. The author has organized them chronologically, in part to show what she observed in compiling them. Trump appears to get worse over time, to become even more nasty, boastful, paranoid and threatening, and even more compulsively driven to tweet around the clock. Some of his most off-the hook Tweets came in at three a.m., when all good non-hypomanics are supposed to be asleep. When that proverbial three a.m. phone call comes in, you don't want the president to be awake, agitated, irritated, and in the middle of a Twitter rant. Most likely at that moment he is causing a crisis of his own making. And if the world also happens to be having a crisis at that moment, is this the man equipped to solve it?

In *The Heart of Man,* Fromm argues that malignant narcissism "lies on the borderline between sanity and insanity."[37] In more benign forms of narcissism, "being related to reality curbs the narcissism and keeps it within bounds," but the malignant narcissist recognizes no such boundaries. With the magnetic force of his will and personality he bends reality to fit his grandiose fantasy.

The thing that distinguishes the malignant narcissistic leader from other patients we might diagnose as having grandiose (biggest crowd size) and persecutory (Obama wiretap) delusions is his power to impose those delusions on the populace. Per Fromm, "This Caesarian madness would be nothing but plain insanity were it not for one factor: by his power Caesar has bent reality to his narcissistic fantasies. He has forced everyone to agree he is god, the most powerful and wisest of men—hence his megalomania seems to be a reasonable feeling."[38]

The organization that I founded, Duty To Warn, is comprised of mental health professionals who believe it is their ethical duty to warn the public about Donald Trump's dangerous mental illness. Fifty-two thousand of us have signed a petition requesting Trump be removed under the twenty-fifth amendment for his severe and dangerous mental illness. At a meeting about Duty to Warn at Yale Medical School, a keynote speaker, Robert J. Lifton, warned that malignantly narcissistic leaders can shift and distort reality for an entire society, a process he called "malignant normality." The abnormal becomes normalized and alternate facts, conspiracy theories, racism, denial of science, and delegitimization of the free press become not only acceptable, but the new normal. Trump has the power to impose his madness on the populace, a kind of mass folie à deux. Perhaps we should call it a *folie des millions*?

To drink the Kool-Aid, just open your Twitter feed.

CHAPTER 1

The Obama Saga
(From Birtherism to the ACA)

We should immediately stop sending our beautiful American tax dollars to countries that hate us and laugh at our President's stupidity!

NOV 7, 2014 11:22 AM

I would say that President Barack Obama was Trump's number one Twitter target until he ran against Hillary Clinton. From the Birther Movement through the remainder of Obama's presidency, Trump rode the Republican anti-Obama train from his Twitter feed all the way to the White House. I would also say that Obama-bashing was one of the ways he earned everyday Republicans' trust and, eventually, votes. That's why we're starting with our forty-fourth president:

2011

There usually is an easy solution to every problem. For instance, a lot of our country's problems can be solved in next year's election.

AUG 24, 2011 3:07 PM

What a shock! The U.S. Capitol Christmas tree pays homage @BarackObama but failed to mention Jesus.

DEC 20, 2011 3:12 PM

@BarackObama has a record low 39% Gallup approval rating. Why so high?

AUG 17, 2011 11:40 AM

@BarackObama has sold guns to Mexican drug lords while his DOJ erodes our 2nd Amendment rights.

JUL 18, 2011 12:21 PM

What is better advice- "The Art of the Deal" or "Rules for Radicals"? I know which one @BarackObama prefers.

JUL 14, 2011 5:12 PM

Sharing a Breitbart article:

While @BarackObama tries to push gun control http://bit.ly/p27G2K --He still has not answered for Project Gun Runner http://bit.ly/pdtrOw

JUL 14, 2011 1:41 PM

Obama Care is already having a devastating impact on our economy.

AUG 5, 2011 11:57 AM

Amazing--Obama speaks, market goes DOWN---Trump tells CNBC he's buying stock---market goes UP --- should not be that way!

AUG 16, 2011 1:42 PM

America's debt officially became 100% of our GDP on @BarackObama's 50th birthday---coincidence?

AUG 4, 2011 1:44 PM

Unbelievable how he gets away with it: @BarackObama is flying around on Air Force One, laughing at everybod... (cont) http://deck.ly/~FIdxS

NOV 30, 2011 8:11 AM

If only @Obama was as focused on balancing the budget as he is on weakening Israel's borders then America would be on the path to solvency.

JUL 7, 2011 12:20 PM

Why did @BarackObama and his family travel separately to Martha's Vineyard? They love to extravagantly spend on the taxpayers' dime.

AUG 26, 2011 10:07 AM

Republicans gave Obama a free pass to the White House -- they just don't get it.

AUG 3, 2011 1:45 PM

2012

OPEC has just raised oil to over $102/Barrel. And @BarackObama still won't approve the Keystone Pipeline. Does he want high gas prices?

JAN 10, 2012 4:10 PM

@BarackObama's class warfare rhetoric is taking a backseat for the DNC convention. He is charging $1 Million for a single suite.

FEB 10, 2012 5:06 PM

An 'extremely credible source' has called my office and told me that @BarackObama's birth certificate is a fraud.

AUG 6, 2012 4:23 PM

I wonder why @BarackObama is not going to the NAACP Convention. Is it because he can't answer questions about 14.7% Black unemployment?

JUL 13, 2012 10:38 AM

Shock - @BarackObama's DNC Convention has a $27M deficit and events are starting to be canceled. http://t.co/HoOrtf0z
JUN 26, 2012 11:18 AM

Obama is laughing at Karl Rove & all the losers who spent hundreds of millions of dollars and didn't win one race, including the big one!
DEC 3, 2012 1:05 PM

Even NY Democrats are avoiding @BarackObama's convention http://t.co/SmKsHwIL He is dragging his own party down with him
AUG 17, 2012 12:52 PM

Many Democrats up for reelection in 2012 are skipping the DNC convention in Charlotte http://t.co/Cak0BpR1 Smart politics!
JUN 22, 2012 1:07 PM

A "Lion's List" of Democrats are not attending @BarackObama's DNC Convention. The Democratic Party is in turmoil. http://t.co/8j3bT1cZ
JUN 27, 2012 1:13 PM

.@BarackObama is now taking credit for changing party platform language but he reviewed it prior to the convention http://t.co/2F5BtROF
SEP 6, 2012 11:48 AM

With all the talk of fiscal responsibility at the @DNC convention yesterday, it was ironic that the debt passed $16T.
SEP 5, 2012 12:36 PM

@BarackObama hard at work yesterday shooting a marshmallow cannon in the WH East Room while our country burns. http://bit.ly/wICXjd
FEB 8, 2012 2:27 PM

Why is Obama playing basketball today? That is why our country is in trouble!

NOV 6, 2012 9:48 AM

With our national debt passing $16T during the @DNC convention, @BarackObama has amassed more debt than the first 42 presidents. Scary.

SEP 4, 2012 3:15 PM

Smart move by @BarackObama having Pres. Bill Clinton deliver the @DNC convention keynote.

SEP 4, 2012 2:48 PM

Great speech by my good friend @GovChristie. He did something you won't hear at @BarackObama's convention---tell the truth.

AUG 29, 2012 12:07 PM

2013

Obama' ststement on Egypt was terrible and dumb-now being used by military as a rallying cry-our foreign policy is worst in U.S. history.

AUG 16, 2013 1:28 AM

The only reason President Obama wants to attack Syria is to save face over his very dumb RED LINE statement. Do NOT attack Syria,fix U.S.A.

SEP 5, 2013 6:13 AM

The Obama Administration has a very important duty to provide a budget - and then negotiate! OUR COUNTRY is a laughingstock!

OCT 7, 2013 5:36 AM

This 'deal' @RNC voted for has $41 in tax increases for every $1 in spending cuts. It is pathetic. Obama is laughing at them.

JAN 2, 2013 11:27 AM

Amnesty is suicide for Republicans.Not one of those 12 million who broke our laws will vote Republican.Obama is laughing at @GOP.

MAR 19, 2013 12:19 PM

Obama and the Democrats are laughing at the deal they just made... the Republicans got nothing!

JAN 1, 2013 7:10 AM

2014

As ISIS and Ebola spread like wildfire, the Obama administration just submitted a paper on how to stop climate change (aka global warming).

OCT 13, 2014 10:17 PM

I have been saying for weeks for President Obama to stop the flights from West Africa. So simple, but he refused. A TOTAL incompetent!

OCT 23, 2014 10:31 PM

Our President is a great embarrassment to the U.S. How could anybody be so dumb or know so little as to make the very stupid 5 for 1 swap?

JUN 3, 2014 10:03 PM

Obama opposes sanctions on Iran http://freebeacon.com/national-security/reports-obama-mulling-sanctions-on-israel/ ... They are laughing at Kerry & Obama!

DEC 8, 2014 1:53 PM

2015

BIG NIGHT ON TWITTER TONIGHT. I WILL BE LIVE TWEETING PRESIDENT OBAMA'S SPEECH AT 7:50 P.M. (EASTERN). MUST TALK RADICAL ISLAMIC TERRORISM!

DEC 6, 2015 7:27 PM

Barack Obama

@BarackObama inherited $10.6 Trillion in National Debt---will leave after his first term with the Debt at over $17.6 Trillion.

AUG 25, 2011 11:54 AM

@BarackObama MUST release a budget before @johnboehner begins negotiations on a continuing appropriations resolution.

AUG 29, 2011 12:06 PM

ObamaCare premiums could jump as high as 51% http://t.co/BdBnj4hm99 Terrible for economy. Repeal & Replace with free market solution!

MAY 28, 2015 3:41 PM

Obama is now warning North Korea on the Yongbyon nuclear reactor http://bit.ly/14MGGvK After Syria, our enemies are laughing!

SEP 13, 2013 1:24 PM

Michelle Obama

Michelle Obama made a terrible mistake in Iowa. When endorsing Bruce Braley before a large crowd, she called him Bruce Bailey seven times.

OCT 11, 2014 5:28 AM

Birtherism

Why do the Republicans keep apologizing on the so called "birther" issue? No more apologies--take the offensive!

AUG 27, 2012 10:58 AM

«@johnnyb23390: @realDonaldTrump - the only confidentiality agreement he signed was for his real birth certificate. keep up the great work!»

JAN 14, 2014 11:10 PM

How amazing, the State Health Director who verified copies of Obama's "birth certificate" died in plane crash today. All others lived

DEC 12, 2013 4:32 PM

"@obamafraudulent: @realDonaldTrump @d18mt2 The birth certificate that you forced Obama to show is a computer generated forgery.

SEP 10, 2013 7:26 PM

People should be proud of the fact that I got Obama to release his birth certificate, which in a recent book he "miraculously" found.

AUG 22, 2013 3:41 PM

Why are people upset w/ me over Pres Obama's birth certificate?I got him to release it, or whatever it was, when nobody else could!

AUG 22, 2013 3:41 PM

"@artlab: @realDonaldTrump Still waiting for the apology on the birth certificate thing. You must be kidding joker!

MAY 7, 2013 5:29 PM

Via @Newsmax_Media: Maher Being Sued by Trump Over Birth Certificate Bet on 'Tonight Show' http://t.co/6a1rJoUz

FEB 6, 2013 1:33 PM

Via @FoxNews: "Donald Trump sends Bill Maher birth certificate, awaits $5 million" http://t.co/5c38hlwz

JAN 10, 2013 1:35 PM

Wake Up America! See article: "Israeli Science: Obama Birth Certificate is a Fake" http://t.co/f7esUdSz

SEP 13, 2012 10:40 AM

Obama asked a 7 yr old for his birth certificate. He›s «in your face» because the Republicans dropped the ball. (cont) http://t.co/FufZD79U

SEP 10, 2012 3:18 PM

Media silent when @BarackObama called @MittRomney a murderer & felon. Mitt mentions 'birth certificate' and they go nuts. Double standard!

AUG 28, 2012 8:37 AM

An 'extremely credible source' has called my office and told me that @BarackObama's birth certificate is a fraud. link

AUG 6, 2012 3:23 PM

Read this--@BarackObama's birth certificate "cannot survive judicial scrutiny" because of "phantom numbers" http://t.co/DIv9sLI2

JUL 23, 2012 3:44 PM

Why does HI Revised Statute 338-17.8 allow an HI resident who doesn't have to be US citizen to procure an official Hawaii birth certificate?

JUL 18, 2012 11:06 AM

Congratulations to @RealSheriffJoe on his successful Cold Case Posse investigation which claims @BarackObama's 'birth certificate' is fake

JUL 18, 2012 10:56 AM

Tomorrow we celebrate Independence Day, America's 236th birthday. Here is America's actual birth certificate http://t.co/0Dnwgi5p \

JUL 3, 2012 11:13 AM

So @ReutersPolitics claims that @MittRomney's birth certificate evokes 'controversy' http://t.co/OMpv8F10 Where (cont) http://t.co/b85y89lz

MAY 30, 2012 3:40 PM

My @CNN interview with @wolfblitzercnn where I discuss @BarackObama's 'birth certificate' and why @CNN has low ratings http://t.co/PQwR5XUh

MAY 30, 2012 1:52 PM

Made in America? @BarackObama argues that his long form birth certificate is irrelevant in court.http://bit.ly/HNTQaT

APR 24, 2012 11:35 AM

PM Let's take a closer look at that birth certificate. @BarackObama was described in 2003 as being "born in Kenya." http://t.co/vfqJesJL

MAY 18, 2012 2:31 PM

Andrew Tahmooressi

"@seyjohnny: Obama traded 5 low life's from Gitmo for a soldier who was considered a deserter, but did nothing for the soldier in Mexico"

NOV 2, 2014 8:26 PM

"@Nardokids:I believe you had a huge part in bringing our soldier out of Mexico. As the Mom of an Airman I thank you for your efforts.Thanks

NOV 2, 2014 8:20 PM

«@Stay_on_Green: Andrew Tahmooressi has been freed by Mexico. Obama didn›t do anything. But I think that @realDonaldTrump did.

OCT 31, 2014 8:15 PM

Obama will let Ebola fly into US & drugrunners cross our border daily. But he won't pressure Mexico on Sgt. Tahmooressi. #FreeOurMarine

OCT 21, 2014 2:14 PM

If I were president Sgt. Andrew Tahmooressi would be let out of jail with one phone call. If not,Mexico would pay a price like never before!

OCT 17, 2014 7:47 PM

Can you believe we still have not gotten our Marine out of Mexico. He sits in prison while our PRESIDENT plays golf and makes bad decisions!

SEP 26, 2014 5:35 PM

Every day Mexico continues to hold Sgt. Tahmooressi is an insult to our country

SEP 16, 2014 3:39 PM

Sgt. Thamooressi has been held in Mexico for 115 Days. Mexico has zero respect for our border & our servicemen. Boycott! #freeourmarine

JUL 24, 2014 4:17 PM

Mexico sent USMC Andrew Tahmooressi back to jail after court hearing. Mexico does not respect our border or U.S. Boycott! #FreeOurMarine

JUL 15, 2014 10:04 AM

...Mexico cannot believe what they are getting away with and have absolutely no respect for our leader.

JUL 11, 2014 10:04 AM

Boycott Mexico until they release our Marine. With all the money they get from the U.S., this should be an easy one. NO RESPECT!

JUN 26, 2014 3:07 AM

Why isn't Mexico releasing our Marine. U.S. should come down really hard on them. They have ZERO respect for our so-called "leader"

JUN 20, 2014 6:19 PM

W/ the ransom Obama paid for deserter Bergdhal, getting Mexico to release USMC Sgt Andrew Tahmooressi is much harder. #BringBackOurMarine

JUN 13, 2014 12:48 PM

Jailed USMC Sgt Andrew Tahmooressi should be released immediately. Since when does Mexico care about border security?#BringBackOurMarine

JUN 13, 2014 12:47 PM

Obama can release 5 senior Taliban for a deserter but can't make Mexico release decorated Marine Sgt. Andrew Tahmooressi. Pathetic

JUN 4, 2014 11:48 AM

Obama on China

China is happy to learn that @BarackObama plans to borrow another $300 Billion. @BarackObama is their favorite client.

SEP 8, 2011 12:23PM

Welcome to the new reality. @BarackObama is now letting China buy US banks http://t.co/i1C02ub2 The US government is selling us out.

MAY 10, 2012 10:18 AM

Waste! With a $16T debt and $1T budget deficit, @BarackObama is sending $770M overseas "to fight global warming" http://t.co/op9x8BYl

MAR 30, 2012 12:55 PM

Obama said in his SOTU that "global warming is a fact." Sure, about as factual as "if you like your healthcare, you can keep it."

JAN 30, 2014 1:14 PM

Obama and Keystone

@BarackObama won't approve the Keystone Pipeline so Canada is now looking to sell their oil to China

JAN 17, 2012 6:26 PM

Our ally Canada wants to send their oil down south to us. @BarackObama is forcing Canada to send it west to China.

FEB 17, 2012 3:46 PM

So-Called Obama

The so-called 'moderate' Syrian rebels pledged their allegiance to ISIS after Obama's address. We should not be arming them!

SEP 12, 2014 1:46 PM

Interesting how President Obama is flying around in a Boeing 747 on so-called Earth Day!

APR 22, 2014 9:54 PM

President Obama spends so much time speaking of the so-called Carbon footprint, and yet he flies all the way to Hawaii on a massive old 747.

DEC 19, 2015 2:25 PM

Obama and the Press

President Obama was terrible on @60Minutes tonight. He said CLIMATE CHANGE is the most important thing, not all of the current disasters!

OCT 11, 2015 8:43 PM

AMAZING how the press protected President Obama when he did the so-called comedy routine with Zach G. He looked like a fool - they said cute

MAR 14, 2014 8:09 AM

Back to work for the President to try and keep some dignity for the office and himself. The so-called rebels must be thoroughly confused!

SEP 11, 2013 5:46 AM

Polls show that the hurricane had a huge positive effect for Obama on his win- isn't that ridiculous?

NOV 8, 2012 5:52 PM

Obamacare (The Affordable Care Act)

ObamaCare must be fully repealed or it will destroy America's small businesses.

AUG 30, 2011 1:31 PM

President Obama could totally solve the problem with Putin by demanding that Russia sign on to ObamaCare, thereby destroying their economy!

MAR 18, 2014 5:09 AM

If we could force Russia, China and other competitors to use ObamaCare, we would be able to instantly destroy their great economic success!

NOV 10, 2013 10:11 PM

Iran Deal

.#IranDeal will go down as one of the dumbest & most dangerous misjudgments ever entered into in history of our country—incompetent leader!

JUL 28, 2015 12:17 PM

Do you think Iran would have acted so tough if they were Russian sailors? Our country was humiliated.

JAN 14, 2016 2:25 PM

Iran admits to aiding the Libyan "Rebels" and Ahmadinejad received a letter of thanks - when will Washington learn? http://bit.ly/paSPy1

AUG 29, 2011 11:39 AM

Obama and Russia

While Putin is scheming and beaming on how to take over the World, President Obama is watching March Madness (basketball)!

MAR 20, 2014 7:14 PM

President Obama, be cool, be smart, be sharp and FOCUS (no more March Madness), and you can beat Putinat his own game. IT CAN BE DONE!

MAR 21, 2014 7:25 AM

America is at a great disadvantage. Putin is ex-KGB, Obama is a community organizer. Unfair.

APR 17, 2014 3:44 PM

Obama should meet with Putin snd convince him to do what is good for the U.S. It's called good dealmaking or, simply, leadership! Cajole.

AUG 8, 2013 11:52 PM

Bottom line, I don't think President changed people's minds - must hope for a lifeline from Putin, a very dangerous lifeline at that!

SEP 10, 2013 8:32 PM

The only reason Obama gave a speech last night was because it was on the schedule-Putin is laughing and the reviews have been really bad!

SEP 11, 2013 5:39 AM

This new Russian strategy guarantees victory for the Syrian government-and makes Obama and U.S. look hopelessly bad. President in trouble!

SEP 10, 2013 6:25 PM

The Russians are playing a very smart game. In the meantime they are buying lots of time for Syria and making U.S. look foolish. Dangerous!

SEP 10, 2013 6:09 PM

Russia is sending a fleet of ships to the Mediterranean. Obama's war in Syria has the potential to widen into a worldwide conflict.

SEP 5, 2013 3:45 PM

Wow, Putin is really taking advantage of President Obama. It is important that Obama responds with strength and determination-be smart-cool!

MAR 17, 2014 9:06 PM

Actually Putin doesn't want Alaska because the Environmental Protection Agency will make it impossible for him to drill for oil!

MAR 4, 2014 7:24 AM

CHAPTER 2

They are Laughing at Us!

Lets fight like hell and stop this great and disgusting injustice! The world is laughing at us.

Nov 6, 2012 8:30 PM

"He's/She's/They're/We're a laughingstock" is an ad hominem argument used by both the left and the right to discuss how ridiculous politicians are when they don't agree with their point of view. But Trump takes it to a new level.

China is Laughing at Us

@BarackObama is sure a master delegator. He has sent @Joe_Biden to China. The Chinese are laughing at us. We MUST do better.

Aug 19, 2011 3:51 PM

China just put a tariff on US cars and trucks--22%--China is laughing at our inept leaders. @BarackObama

Dec 16, 2011 3:36 PM

"The Chinese laugh at how weak and pathetic our government is in combating intellectual property theft." (cont) http://tl.gd/g70qiu

MAR 1, 2012 12:28 PM

China talks about the so-called "carbon footprint" and then, behind our leaders backs, they laugh. They could (cont) http://tl.gd/gd1gc2

MAR 12, 2012 11:08 AM

Thanks to @BarackObama rejecting the Keystone XL pipeline, China has become Canada's biggest oil consumer. China is laughing at us!

JUN 13, 2012 11:41 AM

Now the Chinese are planning a war game w/ the Iranians,Syrians & Russians along Syrian coast. http://bit.ly/NMQzPN Laughing at @BarackObama

JUN 19, 2012 12:33 PM

The US government's foreign debt is at a record $5.29T http://bit.ly/NKxE4x China is laughing all the way to the bank.

AUG 17, 2012 11:33 AM

We can't even stop the Norks from blasting a missile. China is laughing at us. It is really sad.

DEC 12, 2012 12:16 PM

The United States better address China's exchange rate before they steal our country and it is too late! China is laughing at us.

FEB 25, 2013 6:54 PM

China is the biggest environmental polluter in the World, by far. They do nothing to clean up their factories and laugh at our stupidity!

MAR 30, 2013 2:30 PM

The Yuan hit another record high against the Dollar. China is laughing at our expense.

APR 2, 2013 12:49 PM

The Chinese must still be laughing at Kerry's trip to China. He got nothing, gave them everything and promised even more.

APR 17, 2013 11:05 AM

China loved Obama's climate change speech yesterday. They laughed! It hastens their takeover of us as the leading world economy

JUN 26, 2013 12:34 PM

The U.S. has appealed ro Russia not to intervene in Ukraine - Russia tells U.S. they will not become involved, and then laughs loudly!

FEB 28, 2014 5:21 AM

A classic - China just signs massive oil and gas deal with Russia giving Russia plenty of ammo to continue laughing in U.S. face.

MAY 19, 2014 10:45 PM

Wow, China exports rise 15% in September. They are laughing at USA!

OCT 13, 2014 6:21 AM

As China and the rest of the World continue to rip off the U.S. economically, they laugh at us and our president over the riots in Ferguson!

NOV 25, 2014 12:07 AM

China wouldn't provide a red carpet stairway from Air Force One and then Philippines President calls Obama "the son of a whore." Terrible!

SEP 6, 2016 6:12 AM

OPEC Laughs at Us/Rips Us Off

Oil is starting to rise again despite the horrible times. OPEC continues to rip us off. Not worth $30. New leadership needed.

AUG 10, 2011 1:25 PM

Crude is at $85 right now – isn't even worth half that. OPEC is ripping us off.

AUG 29, 2011 2:39 PM

Oil is double the price now compared to last year--OPEC is laughing at @BarackObama.

SEP 6, 2011 11:12 AM

US Gov't is on the hook for more than a third of the world's entire debt & we wonder why China & OPEC are laughing all the way to the bank!

JUL 25, 2012 3:15 PM

Why is oil at a record high? OPEC & the oil speculators continue to rip us off

SEP 11, 2013 2:45 PM

Gas prices are soaring. $4.12 in CA. OPEC is laughing at how stupid we are.

AUG 22, 2012 11:49 AM

It's hard to believe that we are rationing gas in NYC. OPEC is laughing all the way to the bank.

NOV 9, 2012 3:06 PM

$5 a gallon gas and we have yet to approve the Keystone XL Pipeline. OPEC is laughing at us.

FEB 19, 2013 4:47 PM

China's top academics are working w/ PLA in cyber-espionage of our state secrets & R&D http://reut.rs/YsY59Y They are laughing at us!

MAR 25, 2013 1:30 PM

Obama's budget spends $2B making our navy ships algae-powered http://thebea.st/YlCezS The strong world is laughing at us.

APR 11, 2013 12:36 PM

China, OPEC and Russia laugh at us. But now thanks to Obama so does Syria. Very sad!

SEP 3, 2013 1:48 PM

China, Russia and Iran are laughing at us. We have weak leaders who are threatening our national security. Dangerous times.

SEP 12, 2013 12:19 PM

The U.S. accidentally air dropped a large shipment of military weapons and supplies right into the middle of ISIS as enemy laughs! Very sad!

OCT 21, 2014 4:34 PM

Lawyers are Laughing

I'd bet the lawyers for the Central Park 5 are laughing at the stupidity of N.Y.C. when there was such a strong case against their "clients"

JUN 22, 2014 4:23 AM

Sudan Laughs at Us

Now a small country like Sudan tells Obama he can't send any more Marines http://bit.ly/QrFBh2 We are a laughing stock.

SEP 18, 2012 7:39 AM

Terrorists Laugh at Us

The terrorists cut off the heads of Americans and laugh, then want to sell us the bodies for $1,000,000. We fight over sleep deprivation!

DEC 11, 2014 11:23 PM

The five Taliban leaders released for a deserter must really be laughing and having a good time right now. They are saying how dumb U.S. is!

JUN 3, 2014 8:08 PM

American Exceptionalism and the Navy Yard shooting do not go hand in hand. Foreign countries, in particular Russia, are mocking the U.S.

SEP 17, 2013 6:26 AM

The Middle East Laughs at Us

The Iranians have just threatened to send warships to our coasts. They laugh at us. We can't allow them to develop nuclear weapons.

SEP 29, 2011 12:51 PM

The Mullahs are laughing at what they think is a very stupid president,@BarackObama has "asked" for Iran to return the drone #TimeToGetTough

DEC 13, 2011 10:40 AM

The Mullahs laughed when @BarackObama "asked" Iran to return our drone--they will show it to China first.

DEC 14, 2011 1:04 PM

We should not attack Syria but if they make the stupid move to do so, the Arab League,whose members are laughing at us, should pay!

SEP 5, 2013 4:07 PM

Iran is toying with our president - buying time and laughing at the stupidity of our leadership. Syria, and now this! What's next?

SEP 5, 2013 4:46 PM

Mexico is Laughing at Us

Mexico is allowing many thousands to go thru their country & to our very stupid open door. The Mexicans are laughing at us as buses pass by.

JUL 10, 2014 12:24 PM

Russia is Laughing at Us

A sad day for America with Snowden being granted asylum in Russia. Putin is laughing at Obama.

AUG 1, 2013 11:47 AM

Obama wanted Putin to reset. Instead, Putin laughed at him and reloaded.

JUL 21, 2014 1:51 PM

Politicians are Laughing at Us

Obama & Democrat leaders did a great disservice by releasing the papers on torture. The world is laughing at us—they think we are fools!

DEC 11, 2014 8:11 AM

Remember, politicians are all talk and NO action. Our country is a laughing stock that is going to hell. The lobbyists & donors control all!

MAY 12, 2015 8:27 PM

The World Laughs at Us

THE ROLLOUT OF OBAMACARE IS A TOTAL DISASTER AND AN EMBARRASSMENT TO OUR COUNTRY. THE WORLD IS WATCHING AND LAUGHING.$635,000,000 WEBSITE!

OCT 19, 2013 2:41 PM

CHAPTER 3

Everybody's Coming to Get Me (Or Us)!

Hope everyone enjoyed their Thanksgiving. But get ready, our country is in big trouble!

Nov 24, 2012 7:23 PM

China's economy is now projected to overtake the US as the world's largest economy by 2027 http://t.co/c5sI2qTe #TimeToGetTough

Nov 21, 2011 10:36 AM

While it's been mentioned that Trump is paranoid, he often uses paranoia to fan the flames of his base. As we'll get to in a later chapter, he often paints himself as the strong savior who will come along and rescue America. He did this long before 2016, as we saw in Chapter 1, stoked by disaffected Internet users on shouldtrumprun.com. Here is where he fans the flames, especially on foreign policy.

Now China is threatening our allies who share defense pacts with us, the latest is the Philippines http://t.co/zOZKQvPY Very aggressive

May 14, 2012 3:11 PM

Now Chinese agents are smuggling our military weapons through rogue US soldiers http://t.co/kr5OVY5Q China loves to cheat!

MAY 30, 2012 1:34 PM

We can't destroy the competitiveness of our factories in order to prepare for nonexistent global warming. China is thrilled with us!

NOV 5, 2012 11:50 AM

Get Snowden back from Russia—he has done tremendous damage to the US & should pay a very heavy price

APR 15, 2014 1:56 PM

Remember, Russia still has Snowden. When are we going to bring that piece of human garbage back home to stand trial? He caused great damage!

APR 18, 2014 6:43 PM

BREAKING NEWS: Obama has just made a trade with Russia. They get Florida, California & our gold supply. We get borscht & a bottle of vodka.

JUN 5, 2014 11:14 AM

I believe Putin will continue to re-build the Russian Empire. He has zero respect for Obama or the U.S.!

MAR 21, 2014 9:03 PM

Not good or smart for Obama to be calling Russia a "regional" power or to mention the concept of a nuclear weapon going off in NYC.

MAR 26, 2014 3:52 AM

Because of President Obama's failed leadership, we have put Vladimir Putin & Russia back on the world stage! --No reason for this

MAR 31, 2014 3:27 PM

Saudi Arabia was "vehemently" against the Iran nuclear deal. Then today they embraced it. What happened? What did we give them to endorse?

SEP 5, 2015 4:33 PM

President Obama just told President Putin how important the Russian air strikes against ISIS have been. I TOLD YOU SO!

NOV 15, 2015 8:03 PM

"@troyconway: Now 2-more IT Firms going over seas? There is a huge difference between a global economy and GREED! #MakeAmericaGreatAgain

JAN 4, 2016 9:22 PM

Univision is Trying to Stop Him

Mexico's court system is a dishonest joke. I am owed a lot of money & nothing happens.

APR 16, 2015 2:41 PM

Mexican gov doesn't want me talking about terrible border situation & horrible trade deals. Forcing Univision to get me to stop- no way!

JUN 25, 2015 9:26 AM

Univision wants to back out of signed @MissUniverse contract because I exposed the terrible trade deals that the U.S. makes with Mexico.

JUN 25, 2015 9:27 AM

@Univision cares far more about Mexico than it does about the U.S. Are they controlled by the Mexican government?

JUN 26, 2015 10:13 AM

See story in Fusion and Huff. Post about rape at the border. Beyond terrible! Isn't Fusion owned by Univision?

JUN 28, 2015 4:12 PM

Vaccines

Massive combined inoculations to small children is the cause for big increase in autism....

Aug 23, 2012 3:22 PM

"@jamandatrtl Her son was over-vaccinated. #CDCwhistleblower #hearthiswell http://t.co/SZiRcSbGVs"Terrible.

Sep 3, 2014 8:49 AM

He clarifies:

To all haters and losers: I am NOT anti-vaccine, but I am against shooting massive doses into tiny children. Spread shots out over time.

Mar 29, 2014 4:11 AM

Ebola

Something very important, and indeed society changing, may come out of the Ebola epidemic that will be a very good thing: NO SHAKING HANDS!

Oct 4, 2014 1:14 PM

Mexico

Our gov't should immediately stop sending $'s to Mexico, no friend, until they release Marine & stop allowing immigrant inflow into U.S.

Jul 10, 2014 11:28 AM

So many people are angry at my comments on Mexico—but face it—Mexico is totally ripping off the US. Our politicians are dummies!

Feb 25, 2015 10:30 AM

The Mexican legal system is corrupt, as is much of Mexico. Pay me the money that is owed me now - and stop sending criminals over our border

Feb 24, 2015 7:47 PM

I have a lawsuit in Mexico's corrupt court system that I won but so far can't collect. Don't do business with Mexico!

FEB 24, 2015 9:54 AM

The Oscars were a great night for Mexico & why not—they are ripping off the US more than almost any other nation.

FEB 24, 2015 9:53 AM

Immigrants

The fight against ISIS starts at our border. 'At least' 10 ISIS have been caught crossing the Mexico border. Build a wall!

OCT 8, 2014 4:26 PM

If a person is #1 at Harvard and comes from Europe or Asia, they can't get into the U.S. From Mexico etc. with a criminal record, no problem

JUL 10, 2014 6:15 PM

More Terrorism

Everyone is now saying how right I was with illegal immigration & the wall. After Paris, they're all on the bandwagon.

NOV 19, 2015 11:30 AM

President Obama said "ISIL continues to shrink" in an interview just hours before the horrible attack in Paris. He is just so bad! CHANGE.

NOV 14, 2015 8:39 AM

Man shot inside Paris police station. Just announced that terror threat is at highest level. Germany is a total mess-big crime. GET SMART!

JAN 7, 2016 8:24 AM

Why does Obama continue to release the worst of the worst from Gitmo?! Look at Paris and wake up!

JAN 7, 2015 4:56 PM

Isn't it interesting that the tragedy in Paris took place in one of the toughest gun control countries in the world?

JAN 7, 2015 5:29 PM

If the people so violently shot down in Paris had guns, at least they would have had a fighting chance.

JAN 7, 2015 5:28 PM

Top suspect in Paris massacre, Sarah Abdeslam, who also knew everything about the Brussels attack, is no longer talking. Weak leaders, sad!

DELETED AFTER 20 MINUTES AT 10:44 PM ON MAR 25, 2016

Do you all remember how beautiful and safe a place Brussels wss. Not anymore, it is from a different world! U.S. must be vigilant and smart!

DELETED AFTER 1 HOUR AT 8:04 AM ON MAR 22, 2016

My heart and prayers go out to all of the victims of the terrible #Brussels tragedy. This madness must be stopped, and I will stop it.

DELETED AFTER 59 SECONDS AT 4:09 PM ON MAR 22, 2016

Five people killed in Washington State by a Middle Eastern immigrant. Many people died this weekend in Ohio from drug overdoses. N.C. riots!

SEP 25, 2016 7:18 PM

A new radical Islamic terrorist has just attacked in Louvre Museum in Paris. Tourists were locked down. France on edge again. GET SMART U.S.

FEB 3, 2017 7:51 AM

CHAPTER 4

We Are Weak, But I Am Strong

I am a very calm person but love tweeting about both scum and positive subjects. Whenever I tweet, some call it a tirade..totally dishonest!

Nov 11, 2012 8:53 AM

We'll cover bullshit in a later chapter.

Right now, here is one of the cornerstones of Trump's victory: for years, he flooded Twitter with the idea that others were weak, but he was strong. While he doesn't outright say it all the time, pointing out the "weaknesses" of his political opponents was done to make him look better. While he has no political experience, he flipped that into a selling point—at least he's not one of our "weak leaders." And as we'll see in later chapters, he treats it as a political game of dodgeball—get those who are weak (or who conservatives don't like/see as weak) out first, and then go for the stronger ones.

First off, a repeated tweet:

So China is ordering us to raise the Debt Limit...How low have we as a nation sunk?

JUL 19, 2011 8:09 AM

So China is ordering us to raise the Debt Limit...How low have we as a nation sunk?

JUL 19, 2011 9:09 AM

China has so much of our debt that they can't put us in default w/o killing themselves---US needs our toughest negotiator---and fast!

JUL 27, 2011 9:42 AM

China has so much of our debt that they can't put us in default w/o killing themselves---US needs our toughest negotiator---and fast!

JUL 27, 2011 8:42 AM

Trump often uses repetition to drive points home.

@KarlRove's @CrossroadsGPS new ad criticizes Obama for his excessive spending and debt, borrowing from China. Didn't Bush do the same thing?

JUL 28, 2011 12:56 PM

China demanded that we raise our debt ceiling and then their rating agency downgraded us. Our leaders are hope...(less)

AUG 4, 2011 3:09 PM

China's corporate espionage is a continued threat to the American economy. With the right leadership, it can be stopped.

AUG 25, 2011 1:16 PM

Our next President must stop China's Rip-off of America

SEP 21, 2011 10:02 AM

Our deficit spending is China's gain. @BarackObama is bankrupting our country.

SEP 23, 2011 10:17 AM

@BarackObama delayed the Keystone pipeline decision until 2013. Now Canada is looking to export more oil to China.

NOV 14, 2011 4:55 PM

As of September 30th, we have a record trade deficit with China of over $217Billion. They are ripping us off. #TimeToGetTough

NOV 22, 2011 2:08 PM

China is so brazen that they now give us economic advice--they tell us what to do---much like a strong stockh... (cont) http://t.co/wIr68Cn4

NOV 30, 2011 2:25 PM

#TimeToGetTough: Making America #1 Again--my new book--available today. The book both China and OPEC do NOT want you to read.

DEC 5, 2011 11:47 AM

When will the US government finally classify China as a currency manipulator? China is robbing us blind and @BarackObama defends them.

DEC 30, 2011 1:47 PM

Very resource rich Canada, our neighbor, is looking to China for its growth. Just another sad commentary on the U.S. http://t.co/8DUw3buf

MAY 14, 2012 1:19 PM

China is now given preference to buy US debt by going directly to Treasury. I don't believe @BarackObama knows that he selling us out.

MAY 22, 2012 2:41 PM

... to OPEC countries that hate our guts. It's stupid policy."- Time To Get Tough

JAN 15, 2013 3:09 PM

Isn't it sad the way Putin is toying with Obama regarding Snowden. We look weak and pathetic. Could not happen with.a strong leader!

AUG 1, 2013 10:49 PM

I am not angry at Russia (or China) because their leaders are far smarter than ours. We need real leadership, and fast,before it is too late

SEP 6, 2013 8:20 AM

Putin's letter is a masterpiece for Russia and a disaster for the U.S. He is lecturing to our President.Never has our Country looked to weak

SEP 12, 2013 5:26 AM

Putin has become a big hero in Russia with an all time high popularity. Obama, on the other hand, has fallen to his lowest ever numbers. SAD

MAR 21, 2014 9:00 PM

Putin has shown the world what happens when America has weak leaders. Peace Through Strength!

APR 28, 2014 2:37 PM

Russia is on the move in the Ukraine, Iran is nuking up & Libya is run by Al Qaeda, yet Obama is busy issuing 'climate change" warnings.

MAY 7, 2014 3:11 PM

Have you been watching how Saudi Arabia has been taunting our VERY dumb political leaders to protect them from ISIS. Why aren't they paying?

AUG 31, 2014 4:51 PM

Mexico is killing the United States economically because their leaders and negotiators are FAR smarter than ours. But nobody beats Trump!
JUN 19, 2015 8:54 PM

The leader and negotiators representing Mexico are far smarter and more cunning than the leader and negotiators representing the U.S.!
JUN 27, 2015 12:20 PM

Putin is not feeling too nervous or scared. #DemDebate
OCT 13, 2015 7:45 PM

When will the Democrats, and Hillary in particular, say "we must build a wall, a great wall, and Mexico is going to pay for it?" Never!
DEC 25, 2015 3:45 PM

President Obama & Putin fail to reach deal on Syria - so what else is new? Obama is not a natural deal maker. Only makes bad deals
SEP 5, 2016 8:49 AM

"Making America Great Again"

Saturday's attacks show that failed Obama/Hillary Clinton polices won't keep us safe! I will Make America Safe Again!
DELETED AFTER 10 HOURS AT 9:18 AM ON SEP, 19 2016

See, I told you so:

People are finally beginning to hit China and OPEC. They never give me credit for being the first--by far--but that's okay!
AUG 8, 2012 9:51 AM

Housing prices will be going up big league--a great time to buy-- good luck
SEP 26, 2012 1:19 PM

Gas prices are going up big league—I told you so—payback to OPEC!
FEB 5, 2013 10:04 AM

I said gas prices would sky rocket after election - Opec payback!

FEB 18, 2013 6:36 PM

Russia beat the United States in the Olympics-another Obama embarrassment! Isn't it time that we turn things around and start kicking ass?

FEB 23, 2014 10:01 PM

I have been very consistent and always said that Iraq would fall as soon as the U.S. left. What a terrible waste of lives and money!

JUN 14, 2014 7:10 PM

We should have taken the oil in Iraq, and now our mortal enemies have got it, and with no opposition. Really dumb U.S. pols! I'm so angry!

AUG 4, 2014 9:16 AM

"@RealNinjetta @ErinSiegal @AppSame @Univision http://t.co/QNOuFlufaS My many MEXICAN friends fly to visit Mexico because UNSAFE border"

JUL 2, 2015 1:14 PM

Mexico's biggest drug lord escapes from jail. Unbelievable corruption and USA is paying the price. I told you so!

JUL 12, 2015 4:03 PM

When will people, and the media, start to apologize to me for my statement, "Mexico is sending....", which turned out to be true? El Chapo

JUL 13, 2015 5:59 AM

....likewise, billions of dollars gets brought into Mexico through the border. We get the killers, drugs & crime, they get the money!

JUL 13, 2015 5:53 AM

Mexico's totally corrupt gov't looks horrible with El Chapo's escape—totally corrupt. U.S. paid them $3 billion.

JUL 13, 2015 11:21 AM

Mexican leaders and negotiators are much tougher and smarter than those of the U.S. Mexico is killing us on jobs and trade. WAKE UP!

JUL 3, 2015 6:09 AM

"@BonnieKit: Thank you America Ferrara for supporting lawless criminals from Mexico. One more needless death. 2 innocent lives taken"

JUL 3, 2015 6:16 PM

I was never a fan of Bush 2 FOR MANY REASONS, including the fact that we should never have gone into Iraq but once there, kept the oil! DUMB

MAY 17, 2013 5:25 AM

The biggest winner of Obama's '08 win --- Vladimir Putin. Ultimately he could be tied with Iran after Tehran becomes a nuclear power

APR 21, 2014 2:40 PM

Obama told Medvedev after the '12 reelect, he would "have more flexibility." It was music to Putin's ears.

APR 21, 2014 3:17 PM

After thousands lost and spending two trillion dollars, Iraq (I told you so) is imploding. Really dumb pols put us and kept us there-so sad!

APR 22, 2014 3:50 AM

When I said in an interview that Putin is "not going into Ukraine, you can mark it down," I am saying if I am President. Already in Crimea!

AUG 1, 2016 7:50 AM

Vladimir Putin said today about Hillary and Dems: "In my opinion, it is humiliating. One must be able to lose with dignity." So true!

DEC 23, 2016 7:13 PM

Great move on delay (by V. Putin) - I always knew he was very smart!

DEC 30, 2016 2:41 PM

CHAPTER 5

"Sage" Advice and Rhetorical Questions

Every dollar @BarackObama spends costs $1.40 with interest borrowed from China on our children and grandchildren's backs. CUT-CAP-BALANCE!

JUL 18, 2011 1:51 PM

Wake Up America -- China is eating our lunch.

AUG 3, 2011 9:36 AM

Just saying that he is strong while others are weak or taking advantage of us won't cut it unless he "proves" it, and he knows it. So through Twitter, he outlines to his loyal followers how he will fix America, either through already established conservative talking points or taking them a step further.

If the UN unilaterally grants the Palestinians statehood, then the US should cut off all its funding. Actions have consequences.

AUG 30, 2011 12:03 PM

China's business interests reach far and wide---even domestically within our borders. We need to reassess our relationship.

AUG 30, 2011 2:54 PM

OPEC is ripping us off on oil. We are ripping ourselves off by investing in unproven green energy. #Solyndra

SEP 23, 2011 12:56 PM

If China had a tenth of the natural resources we do then they would already be energy independent. Instead we continue to buy oil from OPEC.

SEP 16, 2011 4:20 PM

China does not negotiate from a position of strength, we simply negotiate against ourselves. We have all the advantages but don't execute

SEP 29, 2011 1:50 PM

The Democrats in the Super Committee want to raise taxes first in deficit talks. Huge mistake. Cut wasteful spending first.

OCT 4, 2011 1:29 PM

China's military buildup is a major threat to the Free World. We must remain resolute and maintain our national defense at all costs.

OCT 17, 2011 8:17 AM

@BarackObama is holding Taiwan's request for 66 advanced F-16's. Wrong message to send to China.

OCT 18, 2011 9:16 AM

Now China is publicly supporting the OWS protests http://t.co/CE-kR8i40. It's time for the protesters to go home.

OCT 18, 2011 1:12 PM

Both @BarackObama and China have embraced OWS. All want the
decline of America. Time for the protesters to go home.

OCT 19, 2011 11:55 AM

Why is crude oil priced at $86/Barrel? OPEC is ripping us off. Not
worth $30/Barrel. America needs new leaders.

OCT 21, 2011 8:23 AM

When will Washington stand up to China. China is manipulating
its currency and stealing our jobs. Washington should move on
legislation.

OCT 26, 2011 2:48 PM

Crude is at $100/Barrel. With the current state of the world econo-
my, how is that possible? OPEC is ripping of… (cont) http://t.co/
BJW5fZyc

NOV 16, 2011 3:50 PM

The Oil Companies collude with OPEC to keep oil artificially over-
valued. They need to be reigned in.

NOV 2, 2011 1:57 PM

Why is @BarackObama delaying the sale of F-16 aircraft to Taiwan?
Wrong message to send to China. #TimeToGetTough

NOV 18, 2011 3:34 PM

Washington will continue to run record deficits into the election.
We are borrowing at a rate of $1.40 from China. Truly unsustainable

NOV 28, 2011 2:31 PM

America's trade deficit with China is one of our greatest national
security threats. Time for Fair Trade. We must produce our own
products

NOV 29, 2011 4:03 PM

When it comes to China, @BarackObama practices "pretty please" diplomacy. He begs and pleads and bows--and it'... (cont)

DEC 1, 2011 8:59 AM

Why doesn't OPEC lower the price of crude to help avert the European crisis? Crude keeps rising during the dow... (cont) http://t.co/seLDvy28

DEC 1, 2011 3:15 PM

We are building China's wealth by buying all their products, even though we make better products in America.

DEC 2, 2011 2:16 PM

We must keep the pressure on @BarackObama's administration to make sure Chen comes to the US. It would be a tragedy to abandon him in China.

MAY 7, 2012 3:04 PM

Gas prices are still too high. We really need to pressure OPEC to lower the price of oil.

MAY 9, 2012 2:15 PM

Don't believe the media stories. OPEC and the Saudis have not been doing us any favors recently with oil outputs. Oil should be $30/barrel.

JUN 12, 2012 1:14 PM

Oil is rising back over $100 barrel. OPEC loves to rip us off. Why shouldn't they--they always get away with it.

AUG 20, 2012 3:57 PM

OPEC is better off than they were 4 years ago. Gas has more than doubled during @BarackObama's term. Outrageous!

SEP 5, 2012 8:36 AM

Oil would be $25 a barrel if our government would let us drill. Our country would be rich again--who needs OPEC.

SEP 19, 2012 11:07 AM

OPEC will use yesterday's attacks on our embassies to raise the price of gas. They are always ripping us off.

SEP 12, 2012 2:13 PM

As I predicted 1 year ago, gasoline prices hit a record high today... OPEC is having a ball at our expense.

SEP 2, 2012 5:19 PM

Gas prices are way too high. With an economy contracting and lower demand, how do OPEC & the speculators get away with this?!

AUG 30, 2012 9:00 AM

Got to do something about these missing chidlren grabbed by the perverts. Too many incidents--fast trial, death penalty.

OCT 8, 2012 9:13 AM

Let's continue to destroy the competitiveness of our factories & manufacturing so we can fight mythical global warming. China is so happy!

NOV 1, 2012 9:23 AM

It's Thursday. How much did OPEC steal from all of us today?

NOV 29, 2012 3:19 PM

Crude is about to pass $90/barrel. The OPEC monopoly must be broken. They are robbing our country blind.

NOV 29, 2012 3:20 PM

The interview with Oprah will cause Lance Armstrong huge legal and financial problems- sometimes it is better to go into a corner and hide.

JAN 17, 2013 11:46 AM

NO MERCY TO TERRORISTS you dumb bastards!

APR 21, 2013 10:47 AM

The Generals and top military brass never wanted a mixer but were forced to do it by very dumb politicians who wanted to be politically C!

MAY 7, 2013 6:13 PM

We're spending a fortune looking for the lost plane with mostly Chinese passengers, and that's OK-but how much are Russia & China spending?

MAR 20, 2014 6:44 PM

Terrible for the economy & middle class, gas has now been over $3/ gallon for a record 1,245 days http://t.co/3ACDKbzdCQ FRACK NOW & FAST!

MAY 23, 2014 1:10 PM

What I am saying is that we never should have been in Iraq in the first place. Bush was terrible, Obama is worse! Make America GREAT again.

JUN 10, 2014 6:45 PM

Middle Eastern countries must participate militarily (no running away) and big league financially in order for us to go in and save them!

SEP 10, 2014 8:31 PM

I like Mexico and love the spirit of Mexican people, but we must protect our borders from people, from all over, pouring into the U.S.

JUN 19, 2015 8:15 PM

I love Mexico but not the unfair trade deals that the US so stupidly makes with them. Really bad for US jobs, only good for Mexico.

JUN 25, 2015 9:27 AM

Only very stupid people think that the United States is making good trade deals with Mexico.Mexico is killing us at the border and at trade!

JUN 27, 2015 12:17 PM

We MUST have strong borders and stop illegal immigration. Without that we do not have a country. Also, Mexico is killing U.S. on trade. WIN!

JUN 30, 2015 7:35 AM

I love the Mexican people, but Mexico is not our friend. They're killing us at the border and they're killing us on jobs and trade. FIGHT!

JUN 30, 2015 7:57 AM

The media must immediately stop calling ISIS leaders "MASTER-MINDS." Call them instead thugs and losers. Young people must not go into ISIS!

NOV 20, 2015 7:50 AM

The Iran deal is terrible. Why didn't we get the uranium stockpile - it was sent to Russia. #SOTU

JAN 12, 2016 9:59 PM

The @USCHAMBER must fight harder for the American worker. China, and many others, are taking advantage of U.S. with our terrible trade pacts

JUN 29, 2016 8:09 AM

The Taliban

The five Taliban leaders released for a deserter must really be laughing and having a good time right now. They are saying how dumb U.S. is!

JUN 3, 2014 10:08 PM

REMEMBER, the terrible 5 for 1 trade whereby the Taliban got back leaders (killers) and we got back a NOTHING, WILL COME BACK TO HAUNT U.S.!

Jun 8, 2014 8:51 AM

Libya

The new Libyan Government should turn over the Lockerbie bomber---now.

Aug 30, 2011 3:00 PM

Libyan Rebels should have given us 50% of the oil in return for our military support---we don't even ask!

Aug 26, 2011 2:58 PM

Neither/Nor

China is neither an ally or a friend--they want to beat us and own our country.

Sep 21, 2011 1:12 PM

China and Jobs

China is stealing our jobs. We need to demand China stop manipulating its currency and end its rampant corporate espionage

Sep 28, 2011 1:28 PM

Russia

We will have to see what Russia's next move will be. They may have given him an out of an embarrassing situation or drove into deeper mess!

Sep 10, 2013 8:25 PM

I just got back from Russia-learned lots & lots. Moscow is a very interesting and amazing place! U.S. MUST BE VERY SMART AND VERY STRATEGIC.

Nov 10, 2013 9:44 PM

Many journalists are honest and great - but some are knowingly dishonest and basic scum. They should.be weeded out!

APR 6, 2015 11:42 PM

Robert Pattinson

After Friday's Twilight release, I hope Robert Pattinson will not be seen in public with Kristen--she will cheat on him again!

NOV 13, 2012 1:15 PM

Everybody wants me to talk about Robert Pattinson and not Brian Williams—I guess people just don't care about Brian!

NOV 9, 2012 4:02 PM

Robert Pattinson is putting on a good face for the release of Twilight. He took my advice on Kristen Stewart...I hope!

NOV 9, 2012 1:36 PM

Miss Universe 2012 Pageant will be airing live on @nbc & @Telemundo december 19th. Open invite stands for Robert Pattinson.

OCT 25, 2012 11:29 AM

Everyone knows I am right that Robert Pattinson should dump Kristen Stewart. In a couple of years, he will thank me. Be smart, Robert.

OCT 22, 2012 3:48 PM

Robert Pattinson should not take back Kristen Stewart. She cheated on him like a dog & will do it again--just watch. He can do much better!

OCT 17, 2012 1:47 PM

CHAPTER 6

Everyone's a Loser (But Me)

China

If China had a tenth of the natural resources we do then they would already be energy independent. Instead we continue to buy oil from OPEC.

Sep 16, 2011 4:20 PM

Another company that the DOE has given money to just filed for bankruptcy. This is how the money we borrow at 40% from China is wasted.

Nov 2, 2011 8:09 AM

I truly believe that our country has the worst and dumbest negotiators of virtually any country in the world.

Nov 28, 2013 5:59 AM

China is closing a massive oil deal w/ Russia, taking advantage of the Ukraine conflict http://t.co/tItkQ0PmZH Smart, unlike our leaders.

Apr 22, 2014 3:37 PM

Record setting cold and snow, ice caps massive! The only Global Warming we should fear is that caused by nuclear weapons - incompetent pols.

FEB 19, 2015 7:33 AM

San Jose Protesters are Losers (But His Aren't)

Many of the thugs that attacked the peaceful Trump supporters in San Jose were illegals. They burned the American flag and laughed at police

JUN 4, 2016 6:04 AM

The Mayor of San Jose did a terrible job of ordering the protection of innocent people. The thugs were lucky supporters remained peaceful!

JUN 4, 2016 8:11 AM

Mexico

When will the U.S. stop sending $'s to our enemies, i.e. Mexico and others.

JUL 10, 2014 2:24 PM

People are really unhappy with the endless security checks at the new World Trade Center. Durst is a terriblemanager. Tenants furious!

DEC 10, 2014 8:15 PM

Mexico's court system corrupt.I want nothing to do with Mexico other than to build an impenetrable WALL and stop them from ripping off U.S.

MAR 5, 2015 7:50 PM

Rodolfo Rosas Moya and his pals in Mexico owe me a lot of money. Disgusting & slow Mexico court system. Mexico is not a U.S. friend.

APR 16, 2015 2:41 PM

Word is that Ford Motor, because of my constant badgering at packed events, is going to cancel their deal to go to Mexico and stay in U.S.

OCT 25, 2015 3:36 PM

NOT A CHAPTER

Complete Bullshit and Blatant Lies

Yes You Did

Boston incident is terrible. We need energy and passion, but we must treat each other with respect. I would never condone violence.

AUG 21, 2015 11:35 AM

Never Went Bankrupt

For all of the haters and losers out there sorry, I never went Bankrupt -- but I did build a world class company and employ many people!

APR 18, 2015 6:21 AM

The ISIS Camp in Mexico

ISIS is operating a training camp 8 miles outside our Southern border http://t.co/P8arBncO0A We need a wall. Deduct costs from Mexico!

APR 17, 2015 8:17 AM

All The Climate Change Bullshit

It snowed over 4 inches this past weekend in New York City. It is still October. So much for Global Warming!

NOV 1, 2011 2:43 PM

In the 1920's people were worried about global cooling--it never happened. Now it's global warming. Give me a break!

MAY 4, 2012 3:13 PM

Do you believe @algore is blaming global warming for the hurricane?

NOV 1, 2012 9:13 AM

Global warming is based on faulty science and manipulated data which is proven by the emails that were leaked

NOV 2, 2012 11:59 AM

It's extremely cold in NY & NJ—not good for flood victims. Where is global warming?

NOV 5, 2012 10:55 AM

The concept of global warming was created by and for the Chinese in order to make U.S. manufacturing non-competitive.

NOV 6, 2012 2:15 PM

Looks like the U.S. will be having the coldest March since 1996-global warming anyone?????????

MAR 22, 2013 3:07 PM

It's springtime and it just started snowing in NYC. What is going on with global warming?

MAR 25, 2013 1:14 PM

They changed the name from "global warming" to "climate change" after the term global warming just wasn't working (it was too cold)!

MAR 25, 2013 1:15 PM

Wrong, used to be called global warming and when that name didn't work, they deftly changed it to climate change-because it's freezing!

APR 23, 2013 8:45 PM

"@Jenil93_: @realDonaldTrump No melting of ice caps in the degree that global warming predicted. On the contrary increased ice in Antarctica

APR 24, 2013 3:15 AM

Snow and freezing weather all over mid-section of Country. Global warming specialists better start thinking fast!

MAY 1, 2013 8:04 AM

32° in New York - it's freezing! Where the hell is global warming when you need it?

MAY 14, 2013 5:30 AM

It's freezing outside, where the hell is "global warming"??

MAY 25, 2013 6:00 PM

"@OldManConroy: It's called "climate change". No, they changed it to "climate change" when "global warming" wasn't working anymore-too cold!

MAY 25, 2013 7:15 PM

It's 46° (really cold) and snowing in New York on Memorial Day - tell the so-called "scientists" that we want global warming right now!

MAY 27, 2013 6:21 AM

For the disciples of global warming, in 150 summers (years) there have been 20 heat waves as bad or worse than current-this has happened b4!

JUL 18, 2013 6:15 PM

Where's the global warming? 2013 was one of the least extreme years in weather on record

OCT 21, 2013 1:26 PM

I wonder if the Rutgers coach who had the audacity to yell at the player is a proponent of global warming?

Nov 17, 2013 6:31 PM

Snow and ice, freezing weather, in Texas, Arizona and Oklahoma - what the hell is going on with GLOBAL WARMING?

Nov 23, 2013 8:09 AM

They changed the name global warming to climate change because the concept of global warming just wasn't working!

Nov 23, 2013 8:23 PM

The least number of hurricanes in the U.S. in decades. So they change global warming (too cold) to climate change-now what will they call it

Dec 2, 2013 8:46 AM

Denver, Minnesota and others are bracing for some of the coldest weather on record. What are the global warming geniuses saying about this?

Dec 3, 2013 6:42 PM

Wow, record setting cold temperatures throughout large parts of the country. Must be global warming, I mean climate change!

Dec 4, 2013 6:40 PM

Ice storm rolls from Texas to Tennessee - I'm in Los Angeles and it's freezing. *Global warming is a total, and very expensive, hoax!*

Dec 6, 2013 10:13 AM

Ice storm rolls from Texas to Tennessee - I'm in Los Angeles and it's freezing. Global warming is a total, and very expensive, hoax!

Dec 6, 2013 7:13 AM

This is one of the COLDEST WINTERS ever, freezing all over the country for long periods of time! So much for GLOBAL WARMING.

DEC 12, 2013 6:38 AM

Wow, it's snowing in Isreal and on the pyramids in Egypt. Are we still wasting billions on the global warming con? MAKE U.S. COMPETITIVE!

DEC 14, 2013 4:32 PM

Wow, it's snowing in Isreal and on the pyramids in Egypt. Are we still wasting billions on the global warmingcon? MAKE U.S. COMPETITIVE!

DEC 14, 2013 7:32 PM (REPEAT TWEET)

59% of the United States, by area, is now covered in snow-highest % in many years. The "global warming" name isn't working anymore-SORRY!

DEC 15, 2013 4:38 AM

They call it "climate change" now because the words "global warming" didn't work anymore. Same people fighting hard to keep it all going!

DEC 15, 2013 4:58 AM

We should be focusing on beautiful, clean air & not on wasteful & very expensive GLOBAL WARMINGbullshit! China & others are hurting our air

DEC 15, 2013 5:07 AM

It is really too bad that the scientists studying GLOBAL WARMING in Antarctica got stuck on their icebreaker because of massive ice and cold

DEC 27, 2013 7:02 AM

The rescue icebreaker, trying to free the ship of the GLOBAL WARMING scientists, has turned back-the ice is massive (a record). IRONIC!

DEC 28, 2013 7:20 AM

We should be focused on clean and beautiful air-not expensive and business closing GLOBAL WARMING-a total hoax!

DEC 28, 2013 4:30 AM

We should be focused on clean and beautiful air-not expensive and business closing GLOBAL WARMING-a total hoax!

DEC 28, 2013 7:30 AM (REPEAT TWEET)

The global warming scientists don't want to be airlifted off the ship-they are having too much fun and that is too simple a solution-FAME!

DEC 28, 2013 7:37 AM

Temperature at record lows in many parts of the country. 50 degrees below zero with wind chill in large area. Global warming folks iced in!

DEC 29, 2013 6:08 PM

The con artists changed the name from GLOBAL WARMING to CLIMATE CHANGE when GLOBAL WARMINGwas no longer working and credibility was lost!

DEC 30, 2013 7:44 PM

What the hell is going on with GLOBAL WARMING. The planet is freezing, the ice is building and the G.W. scientists are stuck-a total con job

DEC 30, 2013 4:34 PM

This very expensive GLOBAL WARMING bullshit has got to stop. Our planet is freezing, record low temps,and our GW scientists are stuck in ice

JAN 1, 2014 4:39 PM

This very expensive GLOBAL WARMING bullshit has got to stop. Our planet is freezing, record low temps,and our GW scientists are stuck in ice

JAN 1, 2014 7:39 PM (REPEAT TWEET)

"@princebe: Antarctic ice shelf melt 'lowest EVER recorded, global warming is NOT eroding it'

JAN 4, 2014 12:55 AM

We are experiencing the coldest weather in more than two decades-most people never remember anything like this. GLOBAL WARMING anyone?

JAN 6, 2014 6:19 PM

NBC News just called it the great freeze - coldest weather in years. Is our country still spending money on the GLOBAL WARMING HOAX?

JAN 25, 2014 3:48 PM

NBC News just called it the great freeze - coldest weather in years. Is our country still spending money on the GLOBAL WARMING HOAX?

JAN 25, 2014 6:48 PM (REPEAT TWEET)

Snowing in Texas and Louisiana, record setting freezing temperatures throughout the country and beyond. Global warming is an expensive hoax! –

JAN 28, 2014 10:27 PM

Give me clean, beautiful and healthy air - not the same old climate change (global warming) bullshit! I am tired of hearing this nonsense.

JAN 29, 2014 1:44 AM

Watch commodity prices soar because of the freezing cold. Will be bad for the economy. We could use some global warming.

FEB 3, 2014 2:48 PM

When will our country stop wasting money on global warming and so many other truly "STUPID" things and begin to focus on lower taxes?

FEB 5, 2014 3:01 AM

Don't let the GLOBAL WARMING wiseguys get away with changing the name to CLIMATE CHANGE because the FACTS do not let GW tag to work anymore!

FEB 17, 2014 7:39 AM

It's not climate change,it's global warming.Don't let the dollar sucking wiseguys change names midstream because the first name didn't work

FEB 17, 2014 7:38 PM

"@Michael_KSC: @realDonaldTrump @thedropkicks Whether Global Warming or Climate change. The fact is We didn't cause it. We cannot change it.

FEB 18, 2014 3:42 AM

In New York, March was the coldest month in recorded history - we could use some GLOBAL WARMING!

APR 1, 2014 7:06 AM

The global warming we should be worried about is the global warming caused by NUCLEAR WEAPONS in the hands of crazy or incompetent leaders!

MAY 7, 2014 10:53 PM

The only global warming that people should be concerned with is the global warming caused by nuclear weapons because of our weak U.S. leader

JUL 14, 2014 7:22 PM

Tremendous cold wave hits large part of U.S. Lucky they changed the name from global warming to climate change - G.W. just doesn't work!

JUL 16, 2014 7:11 AM

It's late in July and it is really cold outside in New York. Where the hell is GLOBAL WARMING??? We need some fast! It's now CLIMATE CHANGE

JUL 28, 2014 8:47 PM

Windmills are the greatest threat in the US to both bald and golden eagles. Media claims fictional 'global warming' is worse.

SEP 9, 2014 4:19 PM

Wow, 25 degrees below zero, record cold and snow spell. Global warming anyone?

FEB 15, 2015 6:37 PM

Among the lowest temperatures EVER in much of the United States. Ice caps at record size. Changed name from GLOBAL WARMING to CLIMATE CHANGE

FEB 18, 2015 7:17 AM

It's really cold outside, they are calling it a major freeze, weeks ahead of normal. Man, we could use a big fat dose of Global Warming!

OCT 19, 2015 8:30 AM

CHAPTER 7

Frenemies (Once Friends, Now Enemies, Sometimes Friends Again)

Mitt Romney

How will Mitt Romney defend his record on jobs and Romneycare in tonight's debate?

AUG 11, 2011 5:41 PM

I endorsed @MittRomney not because I agree with him on every issue but because he will get tough with China.

FEB 7, 2012 3:23 PM

Why is @MittRomney the only guy who talks about getting tough with China and their currency manipulation?

FEB 8, 2012 1:25 PM

Putin just sent a Russian nuclear sub to the Gulf of Mexico. @BarackObama can't be bothered, he is too concerned with @MittRomney's taxes.

AUG 22, 2012 1:52 PM

Happy to hear that @ralphreed's Faith and Freedom chapters are at the @RNC convention supporting @MittRomney. We must be united to win!

Aug 28, 2012 2:04 PM

"I will implement effective missile defenses to protect against threats. On this, there will be no flexibility with Vladimir Putin." – Mitt

Oct 10, 2012 9:42 AM

Do we still want a President who bows to the Saudis and lets OPEC rip us off? Make America strong, vote for @MittRomney.

Nov 6, 2012 4:16 PM

Why did Mitt Romney BEG me for my endorsement four years ago?

Mar 3, 2016 6:59 AM

These politicians like Cruz and Graham, who have watched ISIS and many other problems develope for years, do nothing to make thing better!

Deleted after 5 minutes at 10:18 AM on Mar 24, 2016

.@MittRomney can only speak negatively about my presidential chances because I have been openly hard on his terrible "choke" loss to Obama!

Oct 18, 2015 10:06 AM

Mitt Romney is a mixed up man who doesn't have a clue. No wonder why he lost! 2/2

Deleted after 14 minutes at 5:09 PM on Mar 18, 2015

Sour Mitt Romney, who ran the worst campaign in presidential history in losing to Obama, is now pushing Kasich. Tell Mitt where to go, vote T

Deleted after 1 hour at 8:13 AM on Mar 15, 2016

When Mitt Romney asked me for my endorsement last time around, he was so awkward and goofy that we all should have known he could not win!

FEB 24, 2016 6:26 PM

Mitt Romney, who was one of the dumbest and worst candidates in the history of Republican politics, is now pushing me on tax returns. Dope!

FEB 25, 2016 7:34 AM

Stuart Stevens is a dumb guy who fails @ virtually everything he touches. Romney campaign,his book,etc. Why does @andersoncooper put him on?

JAN 14, 2016 12:45 AM

CNN

Watch CNN tomorrow at 2 pm & 5 pm and on Friday at 7 pm & 11 pm for a Thanksgiving Special hosted by John King. I'll be a featured guest.

NOV 24, 2010 10:53 AM

(For the rest on CNN, see Chapter 9)

Macy's

My fragrance--"Success"-- is flying off the shelves @Macys. The perfect Christmas gift!

NOV 13, 2012 9:53 AM

Go to Macy's today and buy Trump ties, shirts, suits and cufflinks as a Christmas or holiday present.Great style, great price! ONLY THE BEST

DEC 19, 2013 7:48 AM

When you do your Christmas shopping remember how disloyal @Macys was to the subject of illegal immigration. #BoycottMacys #DumpMacys

NOV 23, 2015 1:45 PM

Good news, disloyal @Macys stock is in a total free fall. Don't shop there for Christmas!

DEC 4, 2015 6:52 PM

Mark Cuban

I watched Mark Cuban on Jay Leno last night - what a jerk!

MAR 14, 2013 6:56 AM

Dummy @mcuban made up a story about a visit to Mar-a-Lago last night on Leno. It never happened—I don't talk that way.

MAR 14, 2013 11:23 AM

I love watching dummy @mcuban promote on ok show named Shark Tank—but he is just a small part of that show.

MAR 14, 2013 1:57 PM

"@ThisNBAgirl: @realDonaldTrump You are not as smart as Mark Cuban, no matter what you think. Keep to what you know. Lets do an I.Q. test!

MAR 18, 2013 4:43 PM

"@OWhiting147: @realDonaldTrump we know you hate Mark Cuban but what are your feelings on Kevin O'Leary?" Never heard of him!

MAR 18, 2013 5:06 PM

"@johnbravo_1: @realDonaldTrump @kmac5911 @mcuban Hey Donald! What's the best confidence builder?" Going against losers like Mark Cuban!

MAR 18, 2013 10:26 PM

"@rodmonium91: @realDonaldTrump Will the Mavs make the playoffs, what do u think Mr Trump?" No, Mark Cuban is a loser!

APR 5, 2013 8:22 AM

"@salesdan48: @realDonaldTrump Mark Cuban is a sad, unhappy man. A facade, masquerading as a Trump wannabe." Very interesting!

APR 11, 2013 7:19 AM

I feel so badly for Mark Cuban-the Dallas Mavericks were just eliminated from the playoffs and his partners are pissed. Very sad!

APR 11, 2013 5:10 AM

"@anthonyskwiat: @QueyNewton @realdonaldtrump ya because mark Cuban is an arrogant punk compared to Donald who's a living legend" Thanks!

APR 17, 2013 7:04 AM

@JeremyPage3011 Mark Cuban can't beat me at anything. He is one of many on Shark Tank and Apprentice has been a much, much bigger show!

MAY 8, 2013 9:16 PM

@mikeluis93 Mark Cuban is a bully who is physically very soft and therefore should immediately stop wearing T shirts. No strength!

MAY 11, 2013 4:35 PM

"@Chuffman48: @realDonaldTrump or should I ask mark Cuban to tweet at me since you wont" He is boring, and much poorer than me!

JUN 30, 2013 7:36 PM

"@davidrhythmguit: @realDonaldTrump @Chuffman48 Mark Cuban accepts the fact that the President of the United States was born here." Doubt it

JUN 30, 2013 8:00 PM

"@Chuffman48: @realDonaldTrump I mean Mark Cuban is better with his money than you" Not even close, dopey.

JUN 30, 2013 7:39 PM

I'm glad that Mark Cuban won the ridiculous case with the S.E.C. It never should have been brought in the first place!

Oct 17, 2013 7:34 AM

"@RivalofElmBlock: @TMZ mark cuban is a nut. way less powerful than Donald Trump" I agree - also, in many ways, a total loser!

Apr 5, 2014 8:03 AM

Major League Baseball was really smart when they wouldn't let Mark Cuban buy a team. Was it his financials or the fact that he's an asshole?

Apr 5, 2014 1:40 PM

"@financeturd: @realDonaldTrump you have many more followers on Twitter than Mark Cuban" I also have far greater wealth and athleticism!

Apr 23, 2014 7:40 AM

If dopey Mark Cuban of failed Benefactor fame wants to sit in the front row, perhaps I will put Gennifer Flowers right alongside of him!

Sep 24, 2016 12:08 PM

If dopey Mark Cuban of failed Benefactor fame wants to sit in the front row, perhaps I will put Jennifer Flowers right alongside of him!

Deleted after 43 minutes at 1:23 PM on Sep 24, 2016
(repeat tweet)

I know Mark Cuban well. He backed me big-time but I wasn't interested in taking all of his calls. He's not smart enough to run for president!

Feb 12, 2017 8:23 AM

Penn Jillete

Penn Jillette shows his dark side in new crowdfunded film Director's Cut

Sep 23, 2013 1:21 PM

I hear @pennjillette show on Broadway is terrible. Not surprised, boring guy (Penn). Without The Apprentice, show would have died long ago.

JUL 16, 2015 5:18 AM

I loved firing goofball atheist Penn @pennjillette on The Apprentice. He never had a chance. Wrote letter to me begging for forgiveness.

JUL 16, 2015 6:10 AM

Whoopi Goldberg

.@WhoopiGoldberg Don't let @Rosie speak badly of you or try to bring you down. She is rude, crude & not smart. She is not in your league.

DEC 1, 2014 3:59 PM

Had a great time yesterday on @theviewtv with @WhoopiGoldberg, @JennyMcCarthy, @SherriEShepherd & guest host @MrJerryOC!

JUN 13, 2014 9:19 AM

.@WhoopiGoldberg had better surround herself with better hosts than Nicole Wallace, who doesn't have a clue. The show is close to death!

JUN 24, 2015 9:07 PM

The @TheView @ABC, once great when headed by @BarbaraJWalters, is now in total freefall. Whoopi Goldberg is terrible. Very sad!

JAN 7, 2016 4:06 PM

Bill O'Reilly

This isn't straight friends-to-enemies. Trump's opinion of O'Reilly seems to swing based on what O'Reilly does for him. Then again, that seems to be his MO for most everyone.

Surprise, @oreillyfactor used my name big league in pre-ads to promote the show—then talked about everyone else but me!

JAN 28, 2015 1:24 PM

@oreillyfactor - bad and very deceptive journalism. Show must be heading in wrong direction, too bad! @SarahPalinUSA

JAN 28, 2015 6:15 PM

.@oreillyfactor was very negative to me in refusing to to post the great polls that came out today including NBC. @FoxNews not good for me!

SEP 21, 2015 5:49 PM

Thank you @oreillyfactor for your wonderful editorial as to why I should have been @TIME Magazine's Person of the Year. You should run Time!

DEC 9, 2015 10:16 PM

.@oreillyfactor please explain to the very dumb and failing @glennbeck that I supported John McCain big league in 2008, not Obama!

JAN 15, 2016 9:02 PM

A big fat hit job on @oreillyfactor tonight. A total waste of time to watch, boring and biased. @brithume said I would never run, a dope!

FEB 22, 2016 6:27 PM

The View

"@kyleraccio: @realDonaldTrump The View was terrible today. I feel sad for ABC!" Rosie killed what was once a very good show - no ratings!

DEC 8, 2014 8:33 PM

I was on The View this morning. We talked about The Apprentice. Tonight's episode is a great one--tough, exciting and surprising. 10 pm/NBC

OCT 28, 2010 2:53 PM

I have been a guest on The View many times when it was successful show. Now the show is dying for lack of ratings. Too bad!

Apr 30, 2015 5:17 AM

The ratings for The View are really low. Nicole Wallace and Molly Sims are a disaster. Get new cast or just put it to sleep. Dead T.V.

Jun 24, 2015 6:55 PM

@TheView T.V. show, which is failing so badly that it will soon be taken off thr air, is constantly asking me to go on. I TELL THEM "NO"

Mar 24, 2016 8:33 AM

Explain how the women on The View, which is a total disaster since the great Barbara Walters left, ever got their jobs. @abc is wasting time

Mar 24, 2016 8:39 AM

Joy Behar, who was fired from her last show for lack of ratings, is even worse on @TheView. We love Barbara!

Jan 7, 2016 1:06 PM

.@WhoopiGoldberg had better surround herself with better hosts than Nicole Wallace, who doesn't have a clue. The show is close to death!

Jun 24, 2015 7:07 PM

The @TheView @ABC, once great when headed by @BarbaraJWalters, is now in total freefall. Whoopi Goldberg is terrible. Very sad!

Jan 7, 2016 1:06 PM

Fox News

My @foxandfriends interview discussing how @BarackObama is running a hateful campaign & the @RNC convention 'Surprise' http://t.co/t4cc60P5

Aug 21, 2012 1:07 PM

I will be on Fox & Friends at 7.00 (20 minutes). Plenty of terrible and tragic news to talk about! Too bad.

JUL 21, 2014 5:42 AM

.@FoxNews you should be ashamed of yourself. I got you the highest debate ratings in your history & you say nothing but bad...

AUG 7, 2015 1:35 PM

"@mimi_saulino: @seanhannity @FoxNews Syrian Muslims escorted into U.S. through Mexico. Now arriving to Oklahoma and Kansas! Congress?"

OCT 12, 2015 10:30 PM

One of the dumbest political pundits on television is Chris Stirewalt of @FoxNews. Wrong facts - check Fox debate rankings, Trump #1. Dope!

NOV 6, 2015 9:20 PM

Between Iraq war monger @krauthammer, dummy @KarlRove, deadpan @GeorgezWill, highly overrated @megynkelly, among others, @FoxNews not fair!

DEC 15, 2015 9:12 AM

Pathetic attempt by @foxnews to try and build up ratings for the #GOPDebate. Without me they'd have no ratings!

JAN 26, 2016 2:43 PM

The statement put out yesterday by @FoxNews was a disgrace to good broadcasting and journalism. Who would ever say something so nasty & dumb

JAN 27, 2016 5:02 AM

Even though every poll, Time, Drudge etc., has me winning the debate by a lot, @FoxNews only puts negative people on. Biased - a total joke!

FEB 14, 2016 7:56 AM

.@FoxNews is so biased it is disgusting. They do not want Trump to win. All negative!

FEB 17, 2016 6:49 AM

Wow, you are all correct about @FoxNews - totally biased and disgusting reporting.

MAR 10, 2016 1:41 PM

"@daybastrop @foxandfriends @BretBaier The liars that signed the pledge and now won't support @realDonaldTrump IS the reason they are losers

MAY 9, 2016 7:15 AM

Wow, @CNN is so negative. Their panel is a joke, biased and very dumb. I'm turning to @FoxNews where we get a fair shake! Mike will do great

OCT 4, 2016 7:12 PM

CBS

Wow, the ratings for @60Minutes last night were their biggest in a year--- very nice!

SEP 28, 2015 3:00 PM

Face The Nation's interview of me was the highest rated show that they have had in 15 years. Congratulations and WOW! @CBSNews @jdickerson

JAN 11, 2016 6:42 PM

.@MajorCBS Major Garrett of @CBSNews covers me very inaccurately. Total agenda, bad reporter!

JAN 11, 2016 5:49 PM

TIME Magazine

I knew last year that @TIME Magazine lost all credibility when they didn't include me in their Top 100...

OCT 26, 2012 7:59 AM

The Time Magazine list of the 100 Most Influential People is a joke and stunt of a magazine that will, like Newsweek,soon be dead. Bad list!

APR 26, 2013 8:54 PM

Just took a look at Time Magazine-looks really flimsy like a free handout at a parking lot! The sad end is coming-just like Newsweek!

MAY 1, 2013 5:50 PM

So biased: @TIME made 'The Protester' as the person of the year. @TIME celebrates OWS but vilified the Tea Party last year.

DEC 15, 2011 12:06 PM

The TIME Magazine cover showing late age breast feeding is disgusting--sad what TIME did to get noticed. @TIME

MAY 14, 2012 7:13 AM

.@TIME Magazine should definitely pick David Pecker to run things over there - he'd make it exciting and win awards!

JUL 9, 2013 4:38 PM

On the cover of @TIME Magazine—a great honor! http://t.co/zlEHp49oPs

AUG 20, 2015 9:57 AM

I told you @TIME Magazine would never pick me as person of the year despite being the big favorite They picked person who is ruining Germany

DEC 9, 2015 8:53 AM

Vladimir Putin

He appears elsewhere in this book, which is why this section is tiny. However, like TIME *and O'Reilly above, his reaction to Putin depends on what he's doing—is he towing Trump's conservative or reactionary talking points, being friendly to one of his ventures, or not?*

Putin has no respect for our President --- really bad body language.

JUN 19, 2012 5:14 PM

Do you think Putin will be going to The Miss Universe Pageant in November in Moscow - if so, will he become my new best friend?

JUN 18, 2013 10:17 PM

Putin re Snowden issue "it is like shearing a pig: there's lots of squealing and little fleece."

JUN 27, 2013 2:59 PM

A sad day for America with Snowden being granted asylum in Russia. Putin is laughing at Obama

AUG 1, 2013 1:47 PM

I'm in Moscow for Miss Universe tonight - picking a winner is very hard, they are all winners. Total sellout of arena. Big night in Russia!

NOV 9, 2013 8:47 AM

Can you imagine what Putin and all of our friends and enemies throughout the world are saying about the U.S. as they watch the Ferguson riot

NOV 25, 2014 2:57 AM

Miss Universe

Congratulations to Miss Mexico, Jimena Navarrete, our new Miss Universe 2010, and congratulations to everyone for a fantastic show.

AUG 24, 2010 9:07 AM

Despite Mexico's interest in again hosting the Miss Universe Pageant, it will be because of Rodolfo Rosas Moya that it will never happen.

MAR 5, 2015 5:52 PM

Because of Rodolfo Rosas Moya, who owes me lots of money, Mexico will never again host the Miss Universe Pageant.

MAR 5, 2015 5:57 PM

Univision wants to back out of signed @MissUniverse contract because I exposed the terrible trade deals that the U.S. makes with Mexico.

JUN 25, 2015 9:27 AM

.@Univision cares far more about Mexico than it does about the U.S. Are they controlled by the Mexican government?

JUN 26, 2015 8:13 AM

Scotland

I'm honored to be presented the award of Doctor of Business Administration Honoris Causa from Robert Gordon University in Aberdeen, Scotland

OCT 6, 2010 9:40 AM

Scotland is beautiful and Trump Internatonal Golf Links-Scotland is progressing beautifully as well. http://bit.ly/bUWWNb

OCT 7, 2010 10:22 AM

Vattenfall, the promoter of the money losing wind farm plan in Aberdeen, Scotland, just took a loss of $4.6 billion after dumb European move

JUL 24, 2013 5:05 AM

Thank you @GolfMagazine for putting my Scotland course on your cover and a Top 100 course in the world. http://t.co/pt4JrevifH

AUG 9, 2013 3:09 PM

.@AlexSalmond of Scotland may be the dumbest leader of the free world. I can't imagine that anyone wants him in office.

OCT 29, 2013 11:23 AM

Both Aberdeen and Turnberry in Scotland, and the soon to open Doonbeg in Ireland, blow Bandon Dunes away. Bandon is a toy by comparison!

OCT 20, 2015 2:49 PM

Michael Forbes

Michael Forbes lives in a pigsty and bad liquor company Glenfiddich gave him Scot of the Year award...

Dec 4, 2012 11:23 AM

How could Michael Forbes get Scot of the Year when he lost—badly—to me & Andy Murray, a true Scot, who won the U.S. Open & Olympic gold?

Dec 4, 2012 3:46 PM

Tell 'Top Scot' Michael Forbes to clean up his property—it is an embarrassment to Scotland.

Dec 5, 2012 12:22 PM

CHAPTER 8

"Haters and Losers"

Dopey @Lord_Sugar I'm worth $8 billion and you're worth peanuts...without my show nobody would even know who you are.

DEC 7, 2012 9:48 AM

Most people on this list are people who "crossed" Trump in some way. They gave him a bad review. They were a part of a lawsuit against him. They tweeted something bad about him. Most people on this list are also famous.

Lawyers

The so called 87 year old "lady" was a vicious and skilled investor who was trying to rip me off with made up facts and a blowhard lawyer.

MAY 23, 2013 7:13 PM

I just beat a lawyer from Yale and a lawyer from Harvard, who teamed up against me, in a major case worth millions ($). They were so dumb!

MAR 13, 2014 11:47 AM

Pigs get slaughtered ... again. Ft Lauderdale plaintiffs must pay me close to $400k in legal fees after Trump trial victory.

DEC 19, 2014 1:43 PM

Danny Zucker and *Modern Family*

I never heard of @DannyZucker until his very dumb and endless tweets started pouring out of insecure mind-but I have a great deal for him!

MAY 24, 2013 5:02 PM

"@DannyZuker: @realDonaldTrump @dannyzucker It's @danny-zuker." As I said, I've never heard of you before!

MAY 24, 2013 5:26 PM

@LukewSavage And dumb people like @DannyZucker.

MAY 24, 2013 5:07 PM

See, dummy Danny Zuker, who I never heard until this, started something that he couldn't finish-gutless and unwilling to take my bet!

MAY 25, 2013 7:07 PM

Just tried watching Modern Family - written by a moron, really boring. Writer has the mind of a very dumband backward child. Sorry Danny!

JUN 12, 2013 8:46 PM

Joe Biden

Just as I predicted, @Joe_Biden was a complete disaster in China. He condoned the Chinese one-child policy an... (cont) http://deck.ly/~sjayl

AUG 24, 2011 10:41 AM

iPhone

I can't believe Apple isn't moving faster to create a larger iPhone screen. Bring back Steve Jobs!

JUL 24, 2013 2:48 PM

@iPhoneTeam Better get a large screen iPhone, and fast, or risk losing even more business. Samsung cannot believe you have not acted! DUMB!

SEP 19, 2013 5:36 AM

I wonder if Apple is upset with me for hounding them to produce a large screen iPhone. I hear they will be doing it soon—long overdue.

MAR 24, 2014 9:18 AM

Boycott all Apple products until such time as Apple gives cellphone info to authorities regarding radical Islamic terrorist couple from Cal

FEB 19, 2016 1:38 PM

Remember, Cruz and Bush gave us Roberts who upheld #Obamacare twice! I am the only one who will #MAKEAMERICAGREATAGAIN

FEB 19, 2016 1:38 PM – *FROM AN IPHONE*

I use both iPhone & Samsung. If Apple doesn't give info to authorities on the terrorists I'll only be using Samsung until they give info

FEB 19, 2016 4:32 PM

Tom Brokaw

Marble mouth @tombrokaw asks "why do we think to have a successful eveving you have to have Donald Trump as your guest of honor?" BORING TOM

APR 27, 2013 4:28 AM

Awards

The Emmys are sooooo boring! Terrible show. I'm going to watch football! I already know the winners. Good night.

SEP 22, 2013 8:34 PM

Tragedies

If the morons who killed all of those people at Charlie Hebdo would have just waited, the magazine would have folded - no money, no success!

JAN 14, 2015 9:13 AM

Charlie Hebdo reminds me of the "satirical" rag magazine Spy that was very dishonest and nasty and went bankrupt. Charlie was also broke!

JAN 14, 2015 9:10 AM

Juan Williams (FOX News Analyst)

.@TheJuanWilliams you never speak well of me & yet when I saw you at Fox you ran over like a child and wanted a picture. Please share pic!

JUL 3, 2015 4:29 PM

Brian Williams

Brian--Thanks dummy--I picked up 70,000 twitter followers yesterday alone. Cable News just passed you in the ratings. @NBCNightlyNews

NOV 7, 2012 12:14 PM

I have long stated that Brian Williams was not a very smart guy - all you have to do is look at his past. Now he has proven me correct!

FEB 10, 2015 6:50 PM

Brian Williams, who is not the nice guy that people think he is, has now become totally irrelevant. He will never again hold court!

FEB 10, 2015 7:26 PM

Mayor Nutter of Philadelphia

.@Mayor_Nutter of Philadelphia, who is doing a terrible job, should be ashamed for using such a disgusting word in referring to me.Low life!

DEC 9, 2015 11:01 AM

Martin Bashir

Apparently @MartinBashir said something about me on his show yesterday. I was surprised to find out he is on TV. Who knew?!

Jan 9, 2013 12:23 PM

Sleazebag @BashirLive has just been forced to resign from @msnbc. His pathetic apology wasn't enough to save his job. @SarahPalinUSA

Dec 4, 2013 12:18 PM

Thanksgiving

HAPPY THANKSGIVING to everyone--I love you all, even my many enemies (sometimes!).

Nov 21, 2012 4:42 PM

Happy Thanksgiving to all--even the haters and losers!

Nov 27, 2013 2:22 PM

"@RafaelMerrydel1: The Carter Family Thanksgiving will be a bit happier as Obama officially becomes the worst President in history."

Nov 26, 2014 6:07 PM

Go out and buy CRIPPLED AMERICA: How to Make America Great Again. Doing really well. Great Thanksgiving or Christmas present!

Nov 10, 2015 11:54 AM

Bill Maher

Dumbass @BillMaher has still not given me the 5 million he committed to charity--- we just presented him with a demand notice.

Jan 17, 2013 11:29 AM

Dummy @BillMaher forgot to say that he made an absolute offer which I accepted. Hopefully, charity gets $5M dollars.

Feb 9, 2013 6:18 PM

I don't know what will happen with the lawsuit against dummy @billmaher but have an obligation to charity to bring it.

FEB 12, 2013 4:17 PM

Everyone should cancel HBO until they fire low life dummy Bill Maher! Get going now and feel good about yourself!

MAR 2, 2013 12:39 AM

It's Thursday. @billmaher is still a very dumb guy--just look at his past.

OCT 31, 2013 3:28 PM

I don't get @billmaher and his terrible show - he is dumb as a rock but tries so hard to pass himself off as a great intellect. Check past!

JUN 28, 2013 11:55 PM

Failing comedian Bill Maher, who I got an accidental glimpse of the other night, is really a dumb guy, just look at his past!

JAN 29, 2014 8:36 PM

Dummy Bill Maher did an advertisement for the failing New York Times where the picture of him is very sad-he looks pathetic, bloated & gone!

DEC 23, 2014 10:09 PM

Dan Priest

"@danrpriest: @realDonaldTrump Just out of curiosity, what makes you care so much about what they think?» I study cowards and stupid people

MAY 24, 2013 5:25 PM

People Who Call Him F*ckface Von Clownstick

Amazing how the haters & losers keep tweeting the name "F**k-face Von Clownstick" like they are so original & like no one else is doing it...

MAY 3, 2013 12:35 PM

Jon Stewart

Jon Stewart is the most overrated joke on television. A wiseguy with no talent. Not smart, but convinces dopes he is! Fading out fast.

MAY 30, 2015 3:25 PM

While Jon Stewart is a joke, not very bright and totally overrated, some losers and haters will miss him and his dumb clown humor. Too bad!

MAY 30, 2015 8:48 PM

All the haters and losers must admit that, unlike others, I never attacked dopey Jon Stewart for his phony last name. Would never do that!

MAY 30, 2015 9:33 PM

For those of you that have conveniently forgotten, dummy Jon Stewart is a bad filmmaker. His last effort was a real bomb (in all ways)!

MAY 31, 2015 12:00 AM

While Jon Stewart is a joke, not very bright and totally overrated, some losers and haters will miss him & his dumb clown humor. Too bad!

JUN 1, 2015 11:19 AM

"@MotherJones: Jon Stewart would have been a terrible host of "Meet the Press" http://t.co/Ih81Rt1Jb8"

OCT 10, 2014 6:47 PM

Hugh Hewitt

Very low ratings radio host Hugh Hewitt asked me about Suleiman, Abu Bake al-Baghdad, Hassan Nasrallah and more - typical "gotcha" questions

SEP 5, 2015 5:14 AM

Why would a very low ratings radio talk show host like Hugh Hewitt be doing the next debate on @CNN. He is just a 3rd rate "gotcha" guy!

Sep 5, 2015 5:20 AM

New York Times Editors

There are many editorial writers that are good, some great, & some bad. But the least talented of all is frumpy Gail Collins of NYTimes.

Mar 17, 2014 2:03 PM

I loved the day Paul Goldberger got fired (or left) as N.Y.Times architecture critic and has since faded into irrelevance. Kamin next!

Jun 22, 2014 1:12 AM

Dope Frank Bruni said I called many people, including Karl Rove, losers-true! I never called my friend @HowardStern a loser- he's a winner!

Jan 19, 2016 6:44 AM

Harry Hurt

How can a dummy dope like Harry Hurt, who wrote a failed book about me but doesn't know me or anything about me, be on TV discussing Trump?

Jul 29, 2015 2:44 PM

People like lawyer Elizabeth Beck and failed writer Harry Hurt & others talk about me but know nothing about me—crazy!

Jul 29, 2015 4:45 PM

Barry Diller

With Barry Diller & Tina Brown in charge, did anyone doubt that @Newsweek would be a massive failure?

Oct 19, 2012 10:46 AM

Little Barry Diller, who lost a fortune on Newsweek and Daily Beast, only writes badly about me. He is a sad and pathetic figure. Lives lie!

OCT 10, 2015 2:36 PM

Chris Matthews

I knew Chris Matthews when he was sane and, quite honestly, wonderful. Now he's gone off the deep end as an Obama surrogate. @hardball_chris

AUG 27, 2012 12:41 PM

.@hardball_chris' very small audience is shrinking rapidly because people finally understand that he is very very dumb!

MAR 20, 2013 10:44 AM

.@hardball_chris is a really dumb guy(and I know him well)—that's why he works swimmingly with our leaders in Washington.

MAR 19, 2013 8:38 AM

Rambling and stumbling @hardball_chris is as dumb as a rock!

MAR 28, 2013 9:06 AM

.@hardball_chris must have the lowest IQ on television—now telling people that domestic terrorists are from the right.

APR 16, 2013 7:19 AM

I've known @hardball_chris for a long time & sadly, he gets dumber each & every year--& started from a very low base.

APR 16, 2013 9:30 AM

I am getting worried about Chris @hardball_chris Matthews. Is he drinking again?

AUG 1, 2013 12:47 PM

Chris @hardball_chris Matthews ratings are at new historic lows. He is single-handedly destroying the entire @msnbc channel.

AUG 1, 2013 12:46 PM

Frank Lutz

.@FrankLuntz works really hard but is a guy who just doesn't have it - a total loser!

AUG 3, 2014 7:22 PM

.@FrankLuntz is a low class slob who came to my office looking for consulting work and I had zero interest. Now he picks anti-Trump panels!

AUG 7, 2015 12:28 AM

.@FrankLuntz, your so-called "focus groups" are a total joke. Don't come to my office looking for business again. You are a clown!

AUG 7, 2015 12:45 AM

.@FrankLuntz is a total clown. Has zero credibility! @FoxNews @megynkelly

JAN 15, 2016 6:18 PM

George Will

George Will is a political moron. Last month he said Romney couldn't win.

OCT 9, 2012 10:43 AM

.@georgewillf is perhaps the most boring political pundit on television. Got thrown off ABC like a dog. At Mar-a-Lago he was a total bust!

APR 17, 2015 7:16 PM

Goofy political pundit George Will spoke at Mar-a-Lago years ago. I didn't attend because he's boring & often wrong—a total dope!

JUN 19, 2015 7:27 AM

George Will, one of the most overrated political pundits (who lost his way long ago), has left the Republican Party. He's made many bad calls

JUN 26, 2016 4:24 AM

Eric Erickson

Small crowds at @RedState today in Atlanta. People were very angry at EWErickson, a major sleaze and buffoon who has saved me time and money

AUG 8, 2015 8:45 PM

Wow, great news! I hear @EWErickson of Red State was fired like a dog. If you read his tweets, you'll understand why. Just doesn't have IT!

OCT 8, 2015 8:57 AM

.@EWErickson is a total low life--- read his past tweets. A dummy with no "it" factor. Will fade fast.

OCT 8, 2015 2:59 PM

.@EWErickson got fired like a dog from RedState and now he is the one leading opposition against me.

MAR 18, 2016 12:08 PM

David Brooks

David Brooks, of the New York Times, is closing in on being the dumbest of them all. He doesn't have a clue.

MAR 6, 2016 12:25 PM

While I have never met @nytdavidbrooks of the NY Times, I consider him one of the dumbest of all pundits- he has no sense of the real world!

MAR 18, 2016 11:11 PM

Reading @nytdavidbrooks of the NY Times is a total waste of time, he is a clown with no awareness of the world around him- dummy!

MAR 18, 2016 11:25 PM

John Oliver

.@thehill John Oliver had his people call to ask me to be on his very boring and low rated show. I said "NO THANKS" Waste of time & energy!

Oct 31, 2015 4:21 PM

John Legere and T-Mobile

.@JohnLegere T-Mobile service is terrible! Why can't you do something to improve it for your customers. I don't want it in my buildings.

Apr 11, 2015 7:03 PM

.@TMobile You service is absolutely terrible - get on the ball! @JohnLegere

Apr 11, 2015 7:10 PM

.@TMobile gives terrible service and has many complaints, just check.

Apr 12, 2015 8:30 AM

.@JohnLegere @TMobile John, focus on running your company, I think the service is terrible! Try hiring some good managers.

Nov 15, 2015 7:57 PM

Arsenio Hall

I hear the very ungrateful @ArsenioHall has a show that is absolutely dying in the ratings. Really too bad!

Apr 3, 2014 7:30 AM

@ArsenioHall just got "fired"—the people spoke, ratings were terrible. The Apprentice brought him back from the dead, but he blew it!

Jun 2, 2014 8:13 AM

The NFL

Roger Goodell must stop apologizing to everyone who will listen and toughen up. His street smart players are laughing at him and the NFL!

SEP 19, 2014 1:40 PM

Veteran's Day

Happy Veterans Day to ALL, in particular to the haters and losers who have no idea how lucky they are!!!

NOV 11, 2013 7:59 AM

Christmas

I'd like to wish all of my friends--and even my many enemies--a very Merry Christmas and Happy New Year

DEC 24, 2013 1:12 PM

To EVERYONE, including all haters and losers, HAPPY NEW YEAR. Work hard, be smart and always remember, WINNING TAKES CARE OF EVERYTHING!

DEC 31, 2014 4:15 PM

Ron Fournier

How do third rate talents with no smarts like @ron_fournier get so much time on television news. Boring guy - really bad for ratings!

APR 12, 2015 5:58 PM

Rich Lowry

@RichLowry is truly one of the dumbest of the talking heads - he doesn't have a clue!

SEP 21, 2015 7:22 PM

Incompetent @RichLowry lost it tonight on @FoxNews. He should not be allowed on TV and the FCC should fine him!

SEP 23, 2015 6:21 PM

Alex Pareene

Lightweight reporter Alex Pareene @pareene is known as a total joke in political circles. Hence, he writes for Loser Salon. @Salon

AUG 15, 2012 11:33 AM

Seth Meyers

Seth Myers is so unnatural and uncomfortable doing his show that you have to feel sorry for him. Bad interviewer, marbles in his mouth!

MAY 2, 2014 7:11 PM

.@sethmeyers Seth can't help it - he is really trying hard but just doesn't have what it takes. Very awkward and insecure!

MAY 2, 2014 7:26 PM

This guy @sethmeyers can't do a simple interview—saw him the other night stumbling & mumbling while trying to interview a guest.

MAY 5, 2014 2:01 PM

That Seth Meyers is hosting the Emmy Awards is a total joke. He is very awkward with almost no talent. Marbles in his mouth!

AUG 25, 2014 5:07 AM

Shepherd Smith

Boy is this guy @ShepNewsTeam tough on me. So totally biased. As a reporter, he should be ashamed of himself! #Trump2016

NOV 13, 2015 1:54 PM

Jeff Zucker (CNN Contributor)

Jeff Zucker failed @NBC and he is now failing @CNN.

SEP 9, 2016 7:42 AM

Michael Smercon

I can't believe that @CNN would waste time and money with @smerconish - he has got nothing going. Jeff Zucker must be losing his touch!

Apr 4, 2014 7:05 PM

David Axelrod (CNN Contributor)

Watched @davidaxelrod on @oreillyfactor and the dog hit me even after I made a big contribution to his charity. I never went bankrupt!

Feb 10, 2015 2:16 AM

Why did @oreillyfactor give @davidaxelrod so much time to sell his third rate book. Bill should have hit stammering David MUCH harder! Waste

Feb 10, 2015 5:29 AM

David Gregory on CNN

.@DavidGregory got thrown off of TV by NBC, fired like a dog! Now he is on @CNN being nasty to me. Not nice!

Mar 29, 2016 8:10 PM

Club for Growth

The president of the pathetic Club For Growth came to my office in N.Y.C. and asked for a ridiculous $1,000,000 contribution. I said no way!

Sep 1, 2015 9:05 PM

When I intelligently turned down The Club For Growth crazy request for $1,000,000, they got nasty. What a waste of money that would have been

Sep 1, 2015 9:15 PM

The phony Club For Growth, which asked me in writing for $1,000,000 (I said no), is now wanting to do negative ads on me. Total hypocrites!

SEP 6, 2015 3:11 PM

People forget, it was Club for Growth that asked me for $1 million. I said no & they went negative. Extortion!

MAR 7, 2016 9:54 PM

The Club for Growth is a very dishonest group. They represent conservative values terribly & are bad for America. https://t.co/ rnGoaprYuA

MAR 7, 2016 9:55 PM

Phony Club For Growth tried to shake me down for one millions dollars, and is now putting out nasty negative ads on me. They are total losers

DELETED AFTER 1 HOUR AT 4:39 PM ON MAR 9, 2016

Phony Club For Growth tried to shake me down for one million dollars, & is now putting out nasty negative ads on me. They are total losers!

MAR 9, 2016 4:46 PM

Club For Growth tried to extort $1,000,000 from me. When I said NO, they went hostile with negative ads. Disgraceful!

MAR 18, 2016 2:57 PM

Club for Growth letter- trying to extort $1,000,000.00 from me. Remember, I said- NO! https://t.co/suIfdiMg0Q

MAR 18, 2016 3:05 PM

The Club For Growth said in their ad that 465 delegates (Cruz) plus 143 delegates (Kasich) is more than my 739 delegates. Try again

MAR 31, 2016 11:29 PM

The Club For Growth,which asked me for $1,000,000 in an extortion attempt, just put up a Wisconsin ad with incorrect math.What a dumb group!

MAR 31, 2016 11:23 PM

Days of Remembrance

"@realDonaldTrump: I would like to extend my best wishes to all, even the haters and losers, on this special date, September 11th."

SEP 11, 2013 8:12 PM

I wish everyone, including the haters and losers, a very happy Easter!

APR 5, 2015 5:24 AM

CHAPTER 9

Fake News!
The War on Journalism

Many journalists are honest and great - but some are knowingly dishonest and basic scum. They should.be weeded out!

APR 6, 2015 11:42 PM

When someone is running for president (or has run and is planning to run again, in the case of when this was tweeted), it's disconcerting. Freedom of the press is a cornerstone of our democracy and to have a president that plays favorites with the press undermines that.

As mentioned in previous chapters, Trump sees the press in terms of what they can do for him, as a service of mutual exchange: if they play along and be nice, and don't say a bad word about him, he will promote them and talk about how great they are, especially if he is on their channel or in some way involved. If they're critical of him, he berates them on Twitter.

Graydon Carter/*Vanity Fair*

.@VanityFair magazine is doing so poorly that they make even @NY-Mag look good. Graydon Carter should've been fired a long time ago.

OCT 21, 2013 11:41 AM

@VanityFair Wow, I just looked at the circulation numbers - Vanity Fair Magazine won't be around much longer, it's really in bad shape!

DEC 8, 2013 10:36 PM

Why does Conde Nast allow dopey Graydon Carter to run bad food restaurants while running failing @VanityFair magazine?

DEC 11, 2013 9:24 AM

Sissy Graydon Carter of failing Vanity Fair Magazine and owner of bad food restaurants has a problem-his V.F. Oscar party is no longer "hot"

MAR 2, 2014 6:07 PM

Wow, Vanity Fair was totally shut out at the National Magazine Awards - it got NOTHING. Graydon Carter is a loser with bad food restaurants!

MAY 2, 2014 6:15 AM

Rapidly failing @VanityFair magazine hits me for my strong stance against Obama's "brilliant" 5 killers for 1 deserter trade. Amazing!

JUN 4, 2014 4:47 AM

.@VanityFair Magazine is doing really poorly. It has gotten worse and worse over the years, and has lost almost all of it's former allure!

NOV 15, 2015 6:39 PM

I have watched sloppy Graydon Carter fail and close Spy Magazine and now am watching him fail at @VanityFair Magazine. He is a total loser!

NOV 15, 2015 6:47 PM

Rumor has it that the grubby head of failing @VanityFair Magazine, "Sloppy" Graydon Carter, is going to be fired or replaced very soon?

Oct 16, 2015 4:33 PM

Fortune Magazine

Few people know that @FortuneMagazine is still in business. Tell your writer Alisa Soloman that I left The Apprentice to run for president

Oct 31, 2015 4:13 PM

And again:

Few people know that @FortuneMagazine is still in business. Tell your writer Alisa Soloman that I left The Apprentice to run for president

Oct 31, 2015 6:13 PM

"@FortuneMagazine: Do successful CEOs sleep less than everyone else? https://t.co/SBkP1QZKEh https://t.co/15ZgyzSr1J"

Nov 21, 2015 6:16 PM

GQ Magazine

Dying @GQMagazine just named me to a list. Too bad GQ is no longer relevant—won't be around long!

Dec 2, 2013 11:53 AM

"@MakeupArtist121: 1984 cover of @realdonaldtrump #GQ #Magazine @ivankatrump ...One of my main idols I look up to!!... http://t.co/HSv8GxXXDp"

Nov 14, 2013 6:17 AM

Wall Street Journal

The ever dwindling @WSJ which is worth about 1/10 of what it was purchased for, is always hitting me politically. Who cares!

Jul 20, 2015 7:25 AM

It's amazing that some of the dumbest people on television work for the Wall Street Journal, in particular a real dope named Charles Lane!

OCT 18, 2015 1:15 PM

When and how are the dummies at the @WSJ going to apologize to me for their totally incorrect Editorial on me. I want "smart" trade deals.

NOV 12, 2015 3:51 AM

The failing @WSJ Wall Street Journal should fire both its pollster and its Editorial Board. Seldom has a paper been so wrong. Totally biased!

FEB 21, 2016 3:52 AM

@WSJ is bad at math. The good news is, nobody cares what they say in their editorials anymore, especially me!

MAR 17, 2016 6:11 AM

Please explain to the dummies at the @WSJ Editorial Board that I love to debate and have won, according to Drudge etc., all 11 of them!

MAR 17, 2016 6:22 AM

FORBES

Dummy writer @Clare_OC from failing @Forbes magazine works so hard to make such trivial license deals look important...

JUL 9, 2015 12:10 PM

Dummy @Clare_OC from failing @Forbes magazine: NASCAR deal was 1 nite ballroom, ESPN was small golf outing...

JUL 9, 2015 12:11 PM

Why does a failed magazine like @Forbes constantly seek out trivial nonsense? Their circulation way down. @Clare_OC

JUL 9, 2015 12:12 PM

New York Times

Frumpy and very dumb Gail Collins, an editorial writer at The New York Times, is so lucky to even have a job. Check her out - incompetent!

MAR 15, 2014 4:31 PM

.@CharlesMBlow Why don't you use new polls instead of the single ancient national poll that was a tiny bit negative. Dishonest reporting!

NOV 2, 2015 10:21 AM

The @nytimes is so poorly run and managed that other family members are looking to take over control. With unfunded liabilities-big trouble!

NOV 25, 2015 5:29 PM

The numbers at the @nytimes are so dismal, especially advertising revenue, that big help will be needed fast. A once great institution-SAD!

NOV 25, 2015 5:51 PM

The dopes at the @nytimes bought the Boston Globe for $1.3 billion and sold it for $1.00. Their great old headquarters-gave it away! So dumb

NOV 25, 2015 8:35 PM

The failing @nytimes should focus on fair and balanced reporting rather than constant hit jobs on me. Yesterday 3 boring articles, today2!

NOV 26, 2015 1:46 PM

Really disgusting that the failing New York Times allows dishonest writers to totally fabricate stories.

JAN 19, 2016 6:44 AM

The failing @nytimes is truly one of the worst newspapers. They knowingly write lies and never even call to fact check. Really bad people!

MAR 13, 2016 11:53 AM

The @nytimes purposely covers me so inaccurately. I want other nations to pay the U.S. for our defense of them. We are the suckers-no more!

APR 10, 2016 6:40 AM

I am happy to hear how badly the @nytimes is doing. It is a seriously failing paper with readership which is way down. Becoming irrelevant!

APR 24, 2016 6:27 PM

How bad is the New York Times—the most inaccurate coverage constantly. Always trying to belittle. Paper has lost its way!

APR 26, 2016 10:43 AM

Everyone is laughing at the @nytimes for the lame hit piece they did on me and women.I gave them many names of women I helped-refused to use

MAY 15, 2016 4:13 AM

Wow, I have had so many calls from high ranking people laughing at the stupidity of the failing @nytimes piece. Massive front page for that!

MAY 15, 2016 12:06 PM

The failing @nytimes is greatly embarrassed by the totally dishonest story they did on my relationship with women.

MAY 16, 2016 3:12 PM

No wonder the @nytimes is failing—who can believe what they write after the false, malicious & libelous story they did on me.

MAY 16, 2016 3:13 PM

How quality a woman is Rowanne Brewer Lane to have exposed the @nytimes as a disgusting fraud? Thank you Rowanne.

MAY 19, 2016 10:29 AM

Failing @NYTimes will always take a good story about me and make it bad. Every article is unfair and biased. Very sad!

MAY 20, 2016 9:11 AM

Yesterday's failing @NYTimes fraudulently shows an empty room prior to my speech, when in fact, it was packed!

JUN 18, 2016 8:01 PM

Just read in the failing @nytimes that I was not aware "the event had to be held in Cleveland" - a total lie. These people are sick!

JUL 2, 2016 4:48 AM

The failing @nytimes has become a newspaper of fiction. Their stories about me always quote non-existent unnamed sources. Very dishonest!

AUG 13, 2016 11:29 AM

The failing @nytimes talks about anonymous sources and meetings that never happened. Their reporting is fiction. The media protects Hillary!

AUG 14, 2016 5:24 AM

The reporting at the failing @nytimes gets worse and worse by the day. Fortunately, it is a dying newspaper.

AUG 19, 2016 5:43 AM

Rolling Stone

Sad thing is Rolling Stone was (is) a dead magazine with big downward circulation and now, for them at last, people are talking about it!

JUL 17, 2013 6:17 PM

Don't talk about Rolling Stone Magazine but, most importantly, don't buy it. This degenerate killed and maimed so many wonderful people!

JUL 17, 2013 8:22 PM

A dishonest slob of a reporter, who doesn't understand my sarcasm when talking about him or his wife, wrote a foolish & boring Trump "hit"

FEB 14, 2014 11:34 PM

They should close down Rolling Stone Magazine after the phony rape charge story. University of Virginia should sue them for big bucks!

DEC 8, 2014 6:50 AM

.@RollingStone admitted their scam. Phony @HuffingtonPost and others are no better-- total joke!

APR 6, 2015 7:35 AM

MSNBC

If these guys have any integrity they'd say no to MSNBC -- a network that few watch and is very negative. @AndrewBreitbart re debate.

DEC 12, 2011 12:19 PM

I bet the dumbest political commentator on television, @Lawrence, will soon be thrown off the air for poor (cont) http://tl.gd/fn4k0a

FEB 3, 2012 7:35 AM

Good move by @MSNBC in downgrading @WeGotEd to a dead weekend spot. This is truly a guy who shouldn't be on tv.

MAR 14, 2013 11:45 AM

Sorry to hear @msnbc was dead last, in the gutter, in their Boston bombing coverage http://bit.ly/15A4Msm   @hardball_chris @Lawrence

APR 22, 2013 11:35 AM

What a shame that @msnbc's ratings have sunk even lower in 2013. Prime time down 50%. @TheRevAl's are (cont) http://tl.gd/n_1rm613d

AUG 29, 2013 11:45 AM

.@Lawrence is the poor man's left wing @oreillyfactor(with no ratings)!

APR 30, 2013 9:19 AM

The ratings of The Cycle on MSNBC, a sad and pathetic show, are way down. If they fired racist moron @Toure, a truly stupid guy, they live!

AUG 30, 2013 12:10 PM

The Associated Press

Associated Press knowingly and inaccurately wrote about Liberty University speech. Shameful reporting...no credibility.

SEP 26, 2012 6:23 PM

.ccolvinj @AP is one of the truly bad reporters---working for an organization that has totally lost its way. Stories are fictional garbage.

NOV 21, 2015 6:31 PM

.@AP continues to do extremely dishonest reporting. Always looking for a hit to bring them back into relevancy—ain't working!

NOV 23, 2015 8:22 AM

.@AP is doing very badly. I can say from experience their reporting is terrible & highly inaccurate. Sadly, they are now irrelevant!

NOV 17, 2015 3:48 PM

BBC

No surprise that @BBC is in a major scandal for shoddy journalism. Any network that air's @antbaxter's garbage has zero credibility.

NOV 12, 2012 12:37 PM

The National Review

Jonah Goldberg @JonahNRO of the once great @NRO #National Review is truly dumb as a rock. Why does @BretBaier put this dummy on his show?

APR 20, 2015 4:21 PM

National Review @NRO may be going out of business because of the really pathetic job being done by @JonahNRO. No talent means death - sad!

APR 20, 2015 7:12 PM

Very few people read the National Review because it only knows how to criticize, but not how to lead.

JAN 21, 2016 7:56 PM

National Review is a failing publication that has lost it's way. It's circulation is way down w its influence being at an all time low. Sad!

JAN 21, 2016 7:56 PM

The late, great, William F. Buckley would be ashamed of what had happened to his prize, the dying National Review!

JAN 21, 2016 7:57 PM

The failing @NRO National Review Magazine has just been informed by the Republican National Committee that they cannot participate in debate

JAN 22, 2016 6:24 AM

The dying @NRO National Review has totally given up the fight against Barrack Obama. They have been losing for years. I will beat Hillary!

JAN 22, 2016 12:47 PM

.@BrentBozell, one of the National Review lightweights, came to my office begging for money like a dog. Why doesn't he say that?

JAN 22, 2016 5:32 PM

Love making correct predictions. National Review is over. http://theweek.com/articles/451963/national- ... review-doomed

JAN 23, 2016 5:39 PM

NBC

Sleepy eyes @chucktodd is an absolute joke of a reporter. He is in the bag for Obama. He can't carry @jack_welch's jock.

OCT 8, 2012 12:39 PM

.@ ChuckTodd just informed us that my interview last week on @ MeetthePress was their highest rated show in 4 years. Congrats!

OCT 10, 2015 11:46 AM

Sleepy eyes @chucktodd—one of the dumbest voices in politics-- is angry that I'm doing @ThisWeekABC.

AUG 9, 2013 7:57 AM

Doesn't dummy @chucktodd realize that when I considered running for president, I filed financial papers showing unbelievable numbers.

AUG 9, 2013 9:57 AM

Word is that @NBCNews is firing sleepy eyes Chuck Todd in that his ratings on Meet the Press are setting record lows. He's a real loser!

JAN 25, 2015 10:48 AM

.@KatyTurNBC, 3rd rate reporter & @SopanDeb @ CBS lied. Finished in normal manner&signed autos for 20min. Dishonest!

DEC 5, 2015 4:36 PM

.@KatyTurNBC & @DebSopan should be fired for dishonest reporting. Thank you @GatewayPundit for reporting the truth. #Trump2016

DEC 5, 2015 4:40 PM

.@meetthepress and @chucktodd did a 1 hour hit job on me today – totally biased and mostly false. Dishonest media!

MAR 6, 2016 10:19 AM

Just watched @meetthepress and how totally biased against me Chuck Todd, and the entire show, is against me. The good news-the people get it!

JUL 3, 2016 10:40 AM

The very dishonest @NBCNews refuses to accept the fact that I have forgiven my $50 million loan to my campaign. Done deal!

JUN 30, 2016 12:29 PM

Joe Scarborough (NBC)

Morning Joe Panel is stealing many of my statements and ideas to better America without giving credit -- the story of my life!

AUG 3, 2011 3:07 PM

John Heilemann, the lightweight reporter begging to be on@morning joe, looks like a timebomb waiting to explode-he's a nervous and sad mess!

MAR 6, 2013 7:33 PM

@morningmika I'm watching Joe (who is 100% correct on Afghanistan) fondling the once great Time Magazine-so sad to see how skimpy it is!

NOV 21, 2013 8:39 AM

Joe Scarborough initially endorsed Jeb Bush and Jeb crashed, then John Kasich and that didn't work. Not much power or insight!

MAY 6, 2016 11:03 AM

I hear @JoeNBC of rapidly fading @Morning_Joe is pushing hard for a third party candidate to run. This will guarantee a Crooked Hillary win.

MAY 6, 2016 11:25 AM

Nobody is watching @Morning_Joe anymore. Gone off the deep end - bad ratings. You won't believe what I am watching now!

JUN 8, 2016 5:08 AM

Morning Joe's weakness is its low ratings. I don't watch anymore but I heard he went wild against Rudy Giuliani and #2A - sad & irrelevant!

AUG 10, 2016 8:36 AM

Some day, when things calm down, I'll tell the real story of @JoeNBC and his very insecure long-time girlfriend, @morningmika. Two clowns!

AUG 22, 2016 4:29 AM

Tried watching low-rated @Morning_Joe this morning, unwatchable! @morningmika is off the wall, a neurotic and not very bright mess!

AUG 22, 2016 4:21 AM

Wonderful @pastormarkburns was attacked viciously and unfairly on @MSNBC by crazy @morningmika on low ratings @Morning_Joe. Apologize!

AUG 26, 2016 7:50 AM

Just heard that crazy and very dumb @morningmika had a mental breakdown while talking about me on the low ratings @Morning_Joe. Joe a mess!

SEP 2, 2016 5:28 AM

NEW YORK MAGAZINE

@NYMag Wow, numbers are really looking bad at New York Magazine. While very boring, it is also very biased. Too bad, was once great!

OCT 19, 2013 4:13 PM

@NYMag Can you imagine a top editor at New York Magazine calling for my death-if they were responsible, he would be fired! Totally biased.

OCT 19, 2013 4:23 PM

@NYMag In every interview New York Magazine has done for years they ask the same question - "What do you think of Donald Trump?" Beggars!

OCT 19, 2013 4:33 PM

Too bad about New York Magazine, but there's a much bigger one out there, currently doing a story on me to get even, that I'll soon discuss!

DEC 3, 2013 6:47 AM

Remember I predicted that New York Magazine would fold and people scoffed? Just announced (N.Y.Post) it lost big $'s & is cutting way back

DEC 3, 2013 6:41 AM

Boring & failing @NYMag's 3rd rate political reporter @jheil had flunky @DanAmira write a totally false report about me today......

MAR 15, 2013 1:27 PM

.@NYMag is a piece of garbage but I think it is very nice & charitable that they employ the no-talent illiterate hack @jonathanchait.

MAY 17, 2013 6:56 AM

I love watching the dishonest writers @NYMag suffer the magazine's failure.

OCT 18, 2013 11:27 AM

No wonder @NYMag is doing so poorly, with an idiot Sr. Editor like @DanAmira, it will only get worse!

OCT 18, 2013 1:06 PM

Palm Beach Post

One of the country's dumbest newspapers—The Palm Beach Post--
should be put to sleep. It's dying. @pbpost

JAN 25, 2013 8:37 AM

Politico

.@politico, which is not read or respected by many, may be the most
dishonest of the media outlets--- and that is saying something.

SEP 24, 2015 2:41 PM

The failing @politico news outlet, which I hear is losing lots of money, is really dishonest!

SEP 24, 2015 2:42 PM

I wonder why somebody doesn't do something about the clowns
@politico and their totally dishonest reporting.

OCT 7, 2015 8:46 AM

.@politico has no power, but so dishonest!

OCT 7, 2015 8:47 AM

I was so happy when I heard that @Politico, one of the most dishonest political outlets, is losing a fortune. Pure scum!

OCT 8, 2015 4:49 PM

Wow, just heard really bad stuff about the failing @politico. How
much longer will they be around? Some very untalented reporters.

OCT 29, 2015 7:06 PM

The money losing @politico is considered by many in the world of
politics to be the dumbest and most slanted of the political sites.
Losers!

OCT 29, 2015 3:47 AM

Why can't @Politico get better reporters than Ben Schreckenger? Guy is a major lightweight with no credibility. So dishonest!

DEC 3, 2015 8:49 AM

It was recently reported that 3rd rate $ losing @Politico is a foil for the Clintons. Questions given to Clinton in advance. No credibility.

DEC 3, 2015 11:31 AM

Wow, @Politico is in total disarray with almost everybody quitting. Good news -- bad, dishonest journalists!

APR 5, 2016 12:25 PM

New Hampshire Union Leader

I predict that dying @UnionLeader newspaper, which has been run into the ground by publisher "Stinky" Joe McQuaid, will be dead in 2 years!

DEC 30, 2015 8:11 PM

Wow @UnionLeader circulation in NH has dropped from 75,000 to around 10—bad management. No wonder they begged me for ads.

JAN 5, 2016 8:53 AM

The failing @UnionLeader newspaper in N.H. just sent The Trump Organization a letter asking that we take ads. How stupid, how desperate!

JAN 7, 2016 3:06 AM

I'm protesting the @UnionLeader from having anything to do w/ ABC debate. Their unethical record doesn't give them the right to be involved!

JAN 9, 2016 10:01 AM

UL has lost all credibility under Joe McQuaid w circulation dropping to record lows. They aren't worthy of representing the great people NH.

JAN 10, 2016 1:06 PM

Union Leader refuses to comment as to why they were kicked out of the ABC News debate like a dog. For starters, try getting a new publisher!

JAN 10, 2016 3:23 PM

So professional of @ABC news to throw out the failing @Union-Leader newspaper from their debate. Paper won't survive, highly unethical!

JAN 11, 2016 7:09 AM

New York Daily News

The dying NY Daily News put out a false report about my kids not wanting me to criticize Obama...totally false!

NOV 24, 2012 4:12 PM

The dying @NYDailyNews asked me to do an Editorial on the Central Park 5 ripoff & then they pretend it was my idea. Loser newspaper!

JUN 23, 2014 10:16 AM

The failing @NYDailyNews which just raised its prices because it's dying, said I wear a "wig" when they know I don't. Dishonest.

JUN 23, 2014 10:17 AM

Only a fool would buy the @NYDailyNews. Loses fortune & has zero gravitas. Let it die!

JUN 17, 2015 8:54 AM

.@NYDailyNews, the dying tabloid owned by dopey clown Mort Zuckerman, puts me on the cover daily because I sell. My honor, but it is dead!

JUN 28, 2015 4:23 PM

Worthless @NYDailyNews, which dopey Mort Zuckerman, is desperately trying to sell, has no buyer! Liabilities are massive!

FEB 10, 2016 4:59 AM

There are no buyers for the worthless @NYDailyNews but little Mort Zuckerman is frantically looking. It is bleeding red ink - a total loser!

FEB 11, 2016 6:13 AM

The failing @NYDailyNews, destroyed by little Morty Zuckerman, is preparing to close and save face by going online. It's dead!

FEB 12, 2016 8:19 AM

New York Post

Wow, I have always liked the @nypost but they have really lied when they covered me in Iowa. Packed house, standing O, best speech! Sad.

JAN 28, 2015 5:45 AM

I guess Rupert Murdoch and the @nypost don't like Donald Trump. Such false reporting about my big hit in Iowa. Even my enemies said "bull."

JAN 28, 2015 6:04 AM

Huffington Post

The Huffington Post is such a loser--it will die just as AOL is dying, What a stupid deal AOL made to buy it!

AUG 16, 2012 10:51 AM

What a dumb mistake AOL made buying the @huffingtonpost. How much longer will Arianna last--I predict not much.

OCT 26, 2012 10:30 AM

Huffington Post is just upset that I said its purchase by AOL has been a disaster and that Arianna Huffington is ugly both inside and out!

APR 20, 2014 4:57 PM

The failing @HuffingtonPost and dopey @ariannahuff are writing so much false junk about me-they just can't get enough! BE CAREFUL.

AUG 12, 2013 6:24 PM

The @HuffingtonPost is a total joke & laughing stock of journalism, as is gross Arianna Huffington. They don't report the facts!

FEB 24, 2015 7:09 AM

As dishonest as @RollingStone is I say @HuffingtonPost is worse. Neither has much money - sue them and put them out of business!

APR 6, 2015 7:00 PM

The liberal clown @ariannahuff told her minions at the money losing @HuffingtonPost to cover me as enterainment. I am #1 in Huff Post Poll.

JUL 18, 2015 6:37 AM

CNN

Watch CNN tomorrow at 2 pm & 5 pm and on Friday at 7 pm & 11 pm for a Thanksgiving Special hosted by John King. I'll be a featured guest.

NOV 24, 2010 10:53 AM

The $10 billion (net worth) is AFTER all debt and liabilities. So simple to understand but @CNN & @CNNPolitics is just plain dumb!

JUL 18, 2015 7:03 AM

Just announced that in the history of @CNN, last night's debate was its highest rated ever. Will they send me flowers & a thank you note?

SEP 17, 2015 10:17 AM

.@CNN should listen. Ana Navarro has no talent, no TV persona, and works for Bush—a total conflict of interest.

NOV 9, 2015 12:03 PM

.@CNN has to do better reporting if it wants to keep up with the crowd.So totally one-sided and biased against me that it is becoming boring

NOV 28, 2015 8:03 PM

When will @CNN get some real political talent rather than political commentators like Errol Louis, who doesn't have a clue! Others bad also.

NOV 30, 2015 4:44 AM

Weak and totally conflicted people like @TheRickWilson shouldn't be allowed on television unless given an I.Q. test. Dumb as a rock! @CNN

DEC 9, 2015 11:24 PM

Why does @CNN bore their audience with people like @secupp, a totally biased loser who doesn't have a clue. I hear she will soon be gone!

DEC 9, 2015 6:25 PM

New Day on CNN treats me very badly. @AlisynCamerota is a disaster. Not going to watch anymore.

JAN 21, 2016 12:36 PM

Wow, @CNN has nothing but my opponents on their shows. Really one-sided and unfair reporting. Maybe I shouldn't do their town-hall tonight!

MAR 29, 2016 6:34 AM

I am watching @CNN very little lately because they are so biased against me. Shows are predictable garbage! CNN and MSM is one big lie!

JUN 5, 2016 2:56 PM

CNN, which is totally biased in favor of Clinton, should apologize. They knew they were wrong.

JUN 23, 3016 12:34 PM

I am watching @FoxNews and how fairly they are treating me and my words, and @CNN, and the total distortion of my words and what I am saying

JUN 13, 2016 8:08 AM

.@FoxNews is much better, and far more truthful, than @CNN, which is all negative. Guests are stacked for Crooked Hillary! I don't watch.

JUL 17, 2016 6:04 AM

Here is another CNN lie. The Clinton News Network is losing all credibility. I'm not watching it much anymore.

JUN 23, 2016 12:35 PM

I heard that the underachieving John King of @CNN on Inside Politics was one hour of lies. Happily, few people are watching - dead network!

JUL 10, 2016 11:58 AM

The ratings at @FoxNews blow away the ratings of @CNN - not even close. That's because CNN is the Clinton News Network and people don't like

JUL 17, 2016 6:09 AM

The @CNN panels are so one sided, almost all against Trump. @FoxNews is so much better and the ratings are much higher. Don't watch CNN!

JUL 24, 2016 1:45 PM

No such meeting or conversation ever happened - a made up story by "low ratings" @CNN.

AUG 10, 2016 1:49 PM

.@CNN is so disgusting in their bias, but they are having a hard time promoting Crooked Hillary in light of the new e-mail scandals.

SEP 3, 2016 1:36 PM

.@CNN is unwatchable. Their news on me is fiction. They are a disgrace to the broadcasting industry and an arm of the Clinton campaign.

SEP 9, 2016 7:37 AM

Washington Post

One of the dumber and least respected of the political pundits is Chris Cillizza of the Washington Post @TheFix. Moron hates my poll numbers

MAY 11, 2015 10:44 PM

Highly untalented Wash Post blogger, Jennifer Rubin, a real dummy, never writes fairly about me. Why does Wash Post have low IQ people?

DEC 1, 2015 12:46 PM

.@JRubinBlogger one of the dumber bloggers @washingtonpost only writes purposely inaccurate pieces on me. She is in love with Marco Rubio?

DEC 4, 2015 12:37 PM

.@RuthMarcus of the @washingtonpost was terrible today on Face The Nation.No focus, poor level of concentration-but correct on Hillary lying

JAN 3, 2016 11:03 AM

And again:

.@RuthMarcus of the @washingtonpost was terrible today on Face The Nation.No focus, poor level of concentration-but correct on Hillary lying

JAN 3, 2016 2:03 PM

The tax scam Washington Post does among the most inaccurate stories of all. Really dishonest reporting.

JAN 22, 2016 3:48 PM

The @WashingtonPost quickly put together a hit job book on me-comprised of copies of some of their inaccurate stories. Don't buy, boring!

AUG 22, 2016 6:02 PM

Stephen Hayes (*Weekly Standard*)

How does failed writer and pundit like @stephenfhayes, with no success and little talent, get away with criticizing candidates.

APR 20, 2015 6:48 AM

.@weeklystandard I know your business is failing but you should try to get writers far better than @stephenfhayes.

APR 20, 2015 10:20 AM

Buzzfeed

@mckaycoppins is a failed and dishonest reporter who refuses to mention the sarcasm in my voice when referring to him or irrelevant buzzfeed

FEB 15, 2014 8:30 PM

Bloggers like McKay Coppins & @BuzzFeed are true garbage with no credibility. Record setting crowds & speech not reported. @PiersMorgan

FEB 18, 2014 11:33 AM

Ben Smith (is that really his last name?) of @BuzzFeed is a total mess who probably got his minion Coppins to do what he didn't want to do?

FEB 18, 2014 5:20 PM

I wonder how much money dumb @BuzzFeed and even dumber Ben Smith loooose each year? They have zero credibility - totally irrelevant and sad!

FEB 18, 2014 6:10 PM

Do you think that very dumb reporter(blogger) McKay Coppins has apologized to his wife for his very inappropriate behavior while in Florida?

FEB 23, 2014 4:41 PM

Des Moines Register

The ultra liberal and seriously failing Des Moines Register is BEG-GING my team for press credentials to my event in Iowa today-but they lie!

JUL 25, 2015 6:16 AM

CHAPTER 10

See, They Agree with Me! (Retweeting or Quoting People and Media Who Agree with Trump)

Hmmm...can you imagine me speaking at the RNC Convention in Tampa?http://t.co/SDZUsknQ That's a speech everyone would watch.

MAY 22, 2012 2:11 PM

It's needless to say that Trump has a lot of fans. Sixty million Americans turned out to vote for him. Often, he will retweet their supportive statements to back up what he says. Or, if he gets an endorsement from a celebrity or network (even if it's not an "endorsement" per se—let's say they are only hosting him for an interview).

Endorsements for Trump (as President)

The great boxing promoter, Don King, just endorsed me. Nice!

JUN 10, 2016 10:10 AM

Don King, and so many other African Americans who know me well and endorsed me, would not have done so if they thought I was a racist!

JUN 11, 2016 7:00 AM

I will be meeting with the NRA, who has endorsed me, about not allowing people on the terrorist watch list, or the no fly list, to buy guns.

JUN 15, 2016 8:50 AM

Thank you to Donald Rumsfeld for the endorsement. Very much appreciated. Clinton's conduct has been "disqualifying."

JUN 23, 2016 8:13 AM

The truly great Phyllis Schlafly, who honored me with her strong endorsement for president, has passed away at 92. She was very special!

SEP 6, 2016 6:00 AM

Great honor to be endorsed by popular & successful @gov_gilmore of VA. A state that I very much want to win-THX Jim! https://t.co/x4Y1TAFHvn

SEP 9, 2016 6:13 PM

Great honor to be endorsed by popular & successful @gov_gilmore of VA. A state that I very much want to win-THX Jim! https://t.co/pI5fEHPBjx

DELETED AFTER 1 MINUTE AT 7:13 PM ON SEP 9, 2016

Henry McMaster, Lt. Governor of South Carolina who endorsed me, beat failed @CNN announcer Bakari Sellers, so badly. Funny!

SEP 9, 2016 12:32 PM

Philly FOP Chief On Presidential Endorsement: Clinton 'Blew The Police Off' https://t.co/ATBY343pS1

SEP 19, 2016 2:52 PM

The @SenTedCruz endorsement was a wonderful surprise. I greatly appreciate his support! We will have a tremendous victory on November 8th.

SEP 24, 2016 7:35 AM

Thank you for your endorsement, @GovernorSununu. #MAGA https://t.co/8BEeQPsuyd

SEP 27, 2016 11:58 AM

Bernie should pull his endorsement of Crooked Hillary after she decieved him and then attacked him and his supporters.

OCT 2, 2016 4:48 PM

Nation's Immigration And Customs Enforcement Officers (ICE) Make First-Ever Presidential Endorsement: https://t.co/eO1UY5N9J1

OCT 5, 2016 8:53 PM

Drugs are pouring into this country. If we have no border, we have no country. That's why ICE endorsed me. #Debate #BigLeagueTruth

OCT 19, 2016 8:22 PM

Honored to receive an endorsement from @SJSOPIO - thank you! Together, we are going to MAKE AMERICA SAFE & GREAT AG... https://t.co/PSTcOei5t1

OCT 24, 2016 1:30 PM

Truly honored to receive the first ever presidential endorsement from the Bay of Pigs Veterans Association. #MAGA... https://t.co/aRdlFkVjAx

OCT 25, 2016 1:27 PM

Endorsements By/For Him

Congratulations to the Miss USA Pageant--it was the #1 telecast of the night among ABC, CBS, NBC and Fox. A great show and a huge success.

JUN 21, 2011 8:58 AM

Via @G_Liberty_Voice by Melody Dareing: "Donald Trump Wants to Build a Wall Between U.S. And Mexico" http://t.co/fpYTPAInv0

JUN 1, 2015 11:45 AM

My @jrg710 interview discussing building a cemetery next to Trump National, the FL primary, @ApprenticeNBC and OPEC http://t.co/4kU9UYYm

FEB 1, 2012 10:23 AM

"China is our enemy--they want to destroy us" -- Redstate Interview

JUL 20, 2011 3:10 PM

#TimeToGetTough: Making America #1 Again--my new book--available today. The book both China and OPECdo NOT want you to read.

DEC 5, 2011 11:47 AM

#TimeToGetTough presents bold solutions on taxes, national security, the debt, dealing with OPEC and Chinaand defeating @BarackObama.

DEC 9, 2011 11:00 AM

"So, I speak badly of China, but I speak the truth and what do the consumers in China want? They want Trump."

FEB 6, 2012 12:44 PM

"Donald Trump could again defy the conventional wisdom of the chattering class in November."-- @Newsmax_Media's cover "The Trump Effect"

AUG 1, 2012 10:42 AM

"@Foshay504: @greta DonaldTrump-Love him! It's time to run America like a business. We've given all our wealth to China n Mexico!! No more!

JUL 25, 2015 9:09 PM

A great article by @NolteNC spelling out the truth on Mexico, trade, the border & illegals. Thank you @BreitbartNews http://t.co/oJnV2OXcEc

JUN 27, 2015 3:09 PM

"@JennaLeeUSA: When asked why he has his own magazine covers on his walls - @realDonaldTrump replies: "It's cheaper than wall paper..." Ha!

SEP 27, 2015 9:32 PM

"@josemen31: @realDonaldTrump this Mexican here loves you man!! Keep doing your thing #mexicolovestrump" Great

OCT 25, 2015 1:56 PM

Fans Who Want Him to Run

"@Josh_Millard16: I'm loving everything DonaldTrump has been saying about the Iranian Nuclear deal, China, Mexico, and the border.Please run

APR 1, 2015 1:24 AM

"@dashing1995: You've said Mexico is not a friend. I agree. USA faces Mexico tomorrow in soccer. @ussoccer could use a shout out from you."

APR 15, 2015 7:08 AM

Trump National Doral

Wow, @GolfMagazine just rated the renovation of The Blue Monster the best of the year. Even better they stated it may be best of all time!

DEC 8, 2014 8:22 PM

Thank you @GolfMagazine for your fantastic review of The Blue Monster at Trump National Doral - "BEST U.S. RESORT RENOVATION" - & "ALL TIME"

DEC 8, 2014 8:27 PM

I would like to thank @GolfMagazine for the really nice review of Trump National Doral - Best Renovation of the Year (and maybe all time).

JAN 7, 2015 7:18 PM

Looking for Father's Day gift? @Miamimagazine named the spa @TrumpDoral one of the best places for men to relax

JUN 12, 2015 12:05 PM

"@funton08: @realDonaldTrump @VenueMagazine_ @Trump-Doral That is beautiful"

JAN 15, 2015 11:04 AM

"@VenueMagazine_: .@realDonaldTrump unveils brand new Red Tiger course at @TrumpDoral- http://t.co/0kyD2jwiAu http://t.co/K0BtAQOeNP"

JAN 15, 2015 10:56 AM

.@VenueMagazine_ highlights the opening of @TrumpDoral's brand new #RedTiger course: http://t.co/vguST5ZWN6

JAN 26, 2015 2:24 PM

How He's Awesome

@macmiller "Donald Trump the Song" gets 16M hits on YouTube. Who wouldn't be flattered?

JUL 12, 2011 4:08 PM

People ask me every day to pose for pictures but the camera never works the first time--they are never prepared or maybe just very nervous!

JUL 27, 2011 4:09 PM

Reporters say it's the Trump Bump---I tell CNBC I am buying stocks--- and the market goes up.

AUG 15, 2011 11:49 AM

There is no comparison between @ApprenticeNBC and Shark Tank in the ratings. The Apprentice beats Shark Tank hands...

FEB 26, 2013 3:23 PM

He Gets High Ratings

Watch as I humiliate a dais full of "talent." #TrumpRoast airs tonight at 10:30/9:30c on Comedy Central http://bit.ly/fugbyy

MAR 15, 2011 10:37 AM

Keep talking about me: use #TrumpRoast to tweet about how good I look on @ComedyCentral tonight at 10:30/9:30c http://bit.ly/hN3jow

MAR 15, 2011 4:28 PM

The Comedy Central Roast of Donald Trump last week was the #1 highest rated Comedy Central Roast ever...it brought in 3.5 milion viewers

MAR 18, 2011 6:17 AM

Last weeks Dateline, which I hosted, was the highest rated Dateline since January!

MAR 17, 2013 3:29 AM

Today in history WrestleMania 23: I shave @VinceMcMahon's hair--highest rated show in WWE history @WrestleFact

APR 1, 2014 12:37 PM

Virginia's highest rated wine by @WineEnthusiast, @trumpwinery is inspired by the regions of Bordeaux & Champagne http://bit.ly/1kY0WAB

JUN 16, 2014 9:39 AM

"@ryanbushby: @realDonaldTrump i bet you have some great ideas on how to turn this country around" I do, big league!

DEC 31, 2014 7:11 PM

Many people think that WM23 @WrestleMania "the battle of the billionaires" was the greatest of all time—set all records

MAR 25, 2015 1:02 PM

Endorsements of His IQ

Losers and haters,even you, as low and dumb as you are, can learn from watching Apprentice and checking out my tweets-you can still succeed!

MAR 3, 2013 6:58 PM

Sorry losers and haters, but my I.Q. is one of the highest -and you all know it! Please don't feel so stupid or insecure,it's not your fault

MAY 8, 2013 9:37 PM

He Went to Wharton!

I went to Wharton, made over $8 billion, employ thousands of people & get insulted by morons who can't get enough of me on twitter...!

FEB 12, 2013 4:34 PM

Money!

Isn't it crazy, I'm worth billions of dollars, employ thousands of people, and get libeled by moron bloggers who can't afford a suit! WILD.

FEB 19, 2014 8:14 AM

He Hits Back With a Vengeance!

When someone attacks me, I always attack back...except 100x more. This has nothing to do with a tirade but rather, a way of life!

NOV 11, 2012 8:56 AM

How come every time I show anger, disgust or impatience, enemies say I had a tantrum or meltdown—stupid or dishonest people?

NOV 12, 2012 3:21 PM

It's amazing that people can say such bad things about me but if I say bad things about them, it becomes a national incident.

JAN 9, 2013 3:24 PM

Winning

When somebody challenges you unfairly, fight back - be brutal, be tough - don't take it. It is always important to WIN!

JUN 27, 2015 10:50 AM

His Golf Stuff

Turn to the Cadillac Wold Golf Championship at Trump National Doral - Great golf being played, Rory leading! @NBC

DELETED AFTER 3 HOURS AT 6:52 PM ON MAR 6

He Goes Big League!

"@Drake4444444: @realDonaldTrump why don't you invest in the USA since you're the greatest Patriot?" I do, big league!

JUL 7, 2013 6:38 PM

"@AngryJesusRants: @realDonaldTrump why do you need so much? Change some lives, feed some hungry" I do, big league!

JUN 29, 2013 6:27 PM

"@GaryRathman: @realDonaldTrump do those jobs provide health insurance?" Yes, big league!

SEP 10, 2013 5:03 AM

People are LOVING the Trump sign on the Chicago building. Big league tweets, letters and calls...

JUN 12, 2014 9:15 AM

"@MTRisner @foxandfriends Looking forward to it. You need a permanent position there." They would like that big league - but I have no time!

NOV 17, 2014 6:34 AM

Father's Day Magazine Plugs

"@FiveStarMagazin: Trump Collection is planning hotels in Dubai, Abu Dhabi, Doha and KSA #AHIC2015 @realDonaldTrump http://t.co/ypfkWM8Cj1"

MAY 7, 2015 8:25 AM

Looking for Father's Day gift? @Miamimagazine named the spa @TrumpDoral one of the best places for men to relax http://t.co/kvQ5Z29BW7

JUN 12, 2015 12:05 PM

Backing Him Up on *NY Mag* Feud

I love watching the dishonest writers @NYMag suffer the magazine's failure.

OCT 18, 2013 1:27 PM

@DanAmira @NYMag A terrible statement like that shows how desperate you and your magazine are. You should be ashamed.

OCT 18, 2013 3:04 PM

"@nyccoins: @DanAmira @realDonaldTrump @NYMag Dan, you are a low life dumb ass! Stupid too, who made you an editor?" A dead magazine!

OCT 18, 2013 5:41 PM

"@milosuperpug: @realDonaldTrump @TormeyPaul @DanAmira @NYMag NO got so irrelevant. TIME OUT far better than ny magazine."

OCT 18, 2013 9:52 PM

More Endorsements From Magazines

"@seenontv66: When will People magazine finally realize that THE sexiest man alive is Donald Trump! You are sexy and adorable! #gotmyvote" T

JAN 28, 2015 10:00 AM

My @TheBrodyFile int. from Iowa on how I would build a wall to secure our Southern Border & deduct costs from Mexico http://t.co/G0m5cYcCgk

MAY 20, 2015 3:22 PM

"@thehill: Donald Trump on Mexico: "I would build a wall like nobody can build a wall" http://t.co/KSasQjervA http://t.co/sVZo-ergra9" True.

MAY 25, 2015 7:18 PM

Mike Huckabee Endorsement

Mike Huckebee, a great guy, said the President should appoint me Treasury Secretary. China and OPEC would not be happy.

AUG 13, 2011 12:20 PM

Fan Retweets

"@Dale26: Mr @realDonaldTrump how come the US doesn't listen 2u whenever u give them advice on how deal with all the problems? They are dumb

APR 13, 2013 7:16 PM

"@ry_connolly: @realDonaldTrump telling it like it is on Fox News right now, Mexico is spitting in Obama's face and he does nothing #legend"

JUL 9, 2014 11:08 PM

"@D The government spends millions to keep bad people to come in via air travel. Now they go through Mexico. Wish DonaldTrump was in charge"

JUN 23, 2014 8:52 PM

"@maathewdavis: Got my Dad a Trump tie from Macy's for Father's Day. he loves it. he says it's the best tie he's ever owned!" Great

JUL 31, 2014 8:54 AM

"@VMilaccio: #DonaldTrump was right about #RosieODonnell. She is a no talent loser who deserves her comeuppance. @realDonaldTrump"

FEB 10, 2015 9:50 PM

"@Gingerxoxoxoxo: "@realDonaldTrump: .@TMobile gives terrible service and has many complaints, just check."@VerizonWireless is the best"

APR 12, 2015 8:38 AM

"@destiny_113: @JohnLegere if @realDonaldTrump says your service is terrible, it probably is. His hotels are the best, impeccable service."

APR 12, 2015 2:41 PM

"@ScottFConroy: Kentucky Derby? More like Kentucky Losers! DonaldTrump is only horse in race that matters for America! Strong, fierce, noble

MAY 2, 2015 5:59 PM

"@FlyOSUBuckeye1:Really hoping you announce a 2016 run soon! @Ford building more factories in Mexico! #EatingOurLunch

MAY 5, 2015 9:31 PM

"@2014_vince: @realDonaldTrump bring jobs back from asia and mexico..vote trump for wage justice

MAY 26, 2015 7:34 PM

"@Bobzilla305: @realDonaldTrump @krauthammer is a progressive making money off of the Conservative viewership" A total loser!

JUN 4, 2015 11:10 PM

"@_Snurk: @realDonaldTrump Love it! Always respect FIGHTERS over overrated loser POLITITIANS!! Inspire GREATNESS! #TRUMP #2016"

JUN 16, 2015 2:30 AM

"@PaulaDuvall2: Before Mr. Trump's Presidential bid, I was leaning toward Walker! Glad I was saved from stepping in something TERRIBLE."

Jul 26, 2015 8:29 PM

"@RubenMMoreno: @realDonaldTrump The biggest loser in the debate was @megynkelly. You can't out trump Do111111111111nald Trump. You will lose!

Aug 7, 2015 2:23 AM

"@MISSTHOT: @realDonaldTrump: Ignore the losers and the haters, you are going to make this country great again"

Sep 12, 2015 6:19 AM

"@WhiteGenocideTM: @realDonaldTrump You always have the best crowds. #MakeAmericaGreatAgain"

Deleted after 2 minutes at 8:25 PM on Feb 10, 2016

Piers Morgan

It was great to appear on Piers Morgan Tonight last night as his first live guest. Piers won the Celebrity Apprentice and he's fantastic.

Feb 10, 2011 1:29 PM

.@piersmorgan Russell has nothing going for himself except for energy & aggression. Without that he would be dead—a first class dummy!

Oct 17, 2014 2:18 PM

"@piersmorgan: 'The greatest slaughter in the history of The Apprentice' - @realDonaldTrump on my victory over @OMAROSA #CelebrityApprentice

Feb 9, 2015 8:18 PM

"@piersmorgan: Donald Trump still dominating all polls, debate, cable news, gossip...everything. The GOP nomination is his, he rarely loses!

Oct 20, 2015 10:47 PM

"@piersmorgan: Jeb Bush was as ineffectual as ever. As always, @David_Gergen calls it right: Trump held them off. #GOPDebate"

FEB 7, 2016 5:50 AM

"@piersmorgan: Trump won that debate. People can huff & puff all they like but he was the best candidate on the night. #GOPDebate

FEB 7, 2016 5:51 AM

CHAPTER 11

"Pigs, Dogs, and Slobs": Trump and Women

I have never seen a thin person drinking Diet Coke.

OCT 14, 2012 2:43 PM

This show was taped just before the terrible Bill Cosby revelations came to light. She still should have asked him for money-goes to charity.

JAN 4, 2015 11:17 PM

You will ask why a lot of these didn't go in Chapter 8 or 9. When Trump goes after women, be it politicians or those who spark his ire, he often goes after their appearance, a thing they said that doesn't have to do with him (Elizabeth Warren's claims about her heritage), or their tone of voice, in addition to how they attacked him personally.

Responses to Accusations

Same failing @nytimes "reporter" who wrote discredited women's story last week wrote another terrible story on me today- will never learn!

JUN 1, 2016 7:21 PM

Won $5,000,000 against Miss Pennsylvania, Sheena Monnin, for her terrible and untrue statements about Miss USA Pageant. Not a nice person!

MAY 7, 2014 8:13 AM

It Was a Pen

Why is this reporter touching me as I leave news conference? What is in her hand??

MAR 29, 2016 3:35 PM

Miss USA (which he owns)

BTW The Miss USA pageant was the highest rated non-sports telecast on the Big 4 networks. Congrats to our newly crowned @Nia_Sanchez_!

JUN 11, 2014 1:27 PM

Miss Universe Lawsuits

I just made a very satisfactory settlement with Univision over the $10,000,000 they owed me for Miss Universe broadcasting rights. All's well

DELETED AFTER 3 HOURS AT 1:38 PM ON FEB 13, 2016

Now that I have settled my litigation with Univision, I look forward to sitting down with their star anchor (not baby) for an interview.

DELETED AFTER 3 HOURS AT 1:36 PM ON FEB 13, 2016

The Daily Beast

At least @TheTinaBeast is consistent. She takes over a magazine and it ends up in the gutter.

SEP 12, 2013 12:51 PM

@TheTinaBeast is claiming that she decided to leave the @thedaily-beast. Sure, just like every other magazine that fired her.

SEP 12, 2013 12:51 PM

Michelle Malkin

How does @michellemalkin get a conservative platform? She is a dummy--just look at her past.

Oct 25, 2012 9:17 AM

@michellemalkin You were born stupid!

Mar 22, 2013 10:10 AM

Barbara Res

I gave a woman named Barber's Res a top construction job when such a thing was unheard of - and the break of a lifetime - now she is nasty!

Deleted after 1 minute at 11:40 PM on May 16

What Barbara Res does not say is that she would call my company endlessly, and for years, trying to get back into my company. I said no.

Deleted after 1 minute at 11:55 PM on May 16

Meghan McCain

.@MeghanMcCain was terrible on @TheFive yesterday. Angry and obnoxious, she will never make it on T.V. @FoxNews can do so much better!

Sep 5, 2015 6:56 AM

Cheri Jacobus

Really dumb @CheriJacobus. Begged my people for a job. Turned her down twice and she went hostile. Major loser, zero credibility!

Feb 5, 2016 6:01 PM

Vicky Ward

Just finished reading a poorly written & very boring book on the General Motors Building by Vicky Ward. Waste of time! @WileyBiz

Oct 13, 2014 9:56 AM

3rd rate writer, Vicky Ward, who begged me for help- see her letters to me.

Oct 17, 2014 10:21 AM

Roseanne Brewer

The @nytimes is so dishonest. Their hit piece cover story on me yesterday was just blown up by Roseanne Brewer, who said it was a lie!

Deleted after 1 hour at 9:06 AM on May 16, 2016

Wow, Rosanne Brewer Lane, the most prominently depicted women in the failing @nytimes story yesterday,is on @foxandfriends saying Times lied

Deleted after 2 hours at 9:06 AM on May 16, 2016

Elizabeth Warren

Goofy Elizabeth Warren is weak and ineffective. Does nothing. All talk, no action -- maybe her Native American name?

May 6, 2016 9:44 PM

Goofy Elizabeth Warren and her phony Native American heritage are on a Twitter rant. She is too easy! I'm driving her nuts.

May 6, 2016 9:44 PM

Goofy Elizabeth Warren, Hillary Clinton's flunky, has a career that is totally based on a lie. She is not Native American.

May 6, 2016 6:16 PM

Let's properly check goofy Elizabeth Warren's records to see if she is Native American. I say she's a fraud!

May 6, 2016 6:16 PM

I hope corrupt Hillary Clinton chooses goofy Elizabeth Warren as her running mate. I will defeat them both.

May 6, 2016 6:15 PM

If it were up to goofy Elizabeth Warren, we'd have no jobs in America—she doesn't have a clue.

MAY 11, 2016 4:07 PM

Isn't it funny when a failed Senator like goofy Elizabeth Warren can spend a whole day tweeting about Trump & gets nothing done in Senate?

MAY 11, 2016 3:41 PM

Goofy Elizabeth Warren lied when she says I want to abolish the Federal Minimum Wage. See media—asking for increase!

MAY 11, 2016 3:22 PM

Our Native American Senator, goofy Elizabeth Warren, couldn't care less about the American worker…does nothing to help!

MAY 11, 2016 3:03 PM

Goofy Elizabeth Warren is now using the woman's card like her friend crooked Hillary. See her dumb tweet "when a woman stands up to you…"

MAY 11, 2016 2:37 PM

If the people of Massachusetts found out what an ineffective Senator goofy Elizabeth Warren has been, she would lose!

MAY 11, 2016 2:18 PM

Goofy Elizabeth Warren didn't have the guts to run for POTUS. Her phony Native American heritage stops that and VP cold.

MAY 11, 2016 12:12 PM

Goofy Elizabeth Warren has been one of the least effective Senators in the entire U.S. Senate. She has done nothing!

MAY 11, 2016 9:18 AM

I find it offensive that Goofy Elizabeth Warren, sometimes referred to as Pocahontas, pretended to be Native American to get in Harvard.

MAY 26, 2016 4:15 PM

Goofy Senator Elizabeth Warren @elizabethforma has done less in the U.S. Senate than practically any other senator. All talk, no action!

MAY 25, 2016 7:31 AM

@elizabethforma Goofy Elizabeth Warren, sometimes known as Pocahontas, bought foreclosed housing and made a quick killing. Total hypocrite!

MAY 25, 2016 7:17 AM

@elizabethforma Goofy Elizabeth Warren, sometimes referred to as Pocahontas because she faked the fact she is native American, is a lowlife!

MAY 25, 2016 12:37 AM

Pocahontas is at it again! Goofy Elizabeth Warren, one of the least productive U.S. Senators, has a nasty mouth. Hope she is V.P. choice.

JUN 10, 2016 7:07 AM

Goofy Elizabeth Warren, sometimes referred to as Pocahontas, pretended to be a Native American in order to advance her career. Very racist!

JUN 11, 2016 6:28 PM

Crooked Hillary is wheeling out one of the least productive senators in the U.S. Senate, goofy Elizabeth Warren, who lied on heritage.

JUN 27, 2016 8:07 AM

Goofy Elizabeth Warren, who may be the least productive Senator in the U.S. Senate, must prove she is not a fraud. Without the con it's over

JUL 16, 2016 11:15 PM

I hope that Crooked Hillary picks Goofy Elizabeth Warren, sometimes referred to as Pocahontas, as her V.P. Then we can litigate her
fraud!

> JUL 17, 2016 7:14 AM

If Goofy Elizabeth Warren, a very weak Senator, didn't lie about her
heritage (being Native American) she would be nothing today. Pick
her H

> JUL 17, 2016 7:24 AM

Elizabeth Warren, often referred to as Pocahontas, just misrepresent-
ed me and spoke glowingly about Crooked Hillary, who she always
hated!

> JUL 25, 2016 10:12 PM

Rosie O'Donnell

I feel sorry for Rosie 's new partner in love whose parents are devastated at the thought of their daughter being with @Rosie--a true
loser.

> DEC 14, 2011 11:45 AM

Rosie O'Donnell's show is "dead"- can't keep going for long with such
poor ratings. @Rosie is a stone cold (cont) http://t.co/Jm3YSf7h

> JAN 17, 2012 10:29 AM

Rosie O'Donnell has failed again. Her ratings were abysmal and
Oprah cancelled her on Friday night. When will (cont) http://t.co/
nDQoTVHP

> MAR 19, 2012 9:18 AM

Rosie O'Donnell should leave Lindsay Lohan alone--@Rosie has bigger problems than Lindsay. Lindsay's mother called my office for help

> APR 30, 2012 11:01 AM

.@Cher attacked @MittRomney. She is an average talent who is out of touch with reality. Like @Rosie O'Donnell, a total loser!

May 10, 2012 10:10 AM

"@ForeverMcIn: @realDonaldTrump how much would it take for you to make out with Rosie O'Donnell?" One trillion, at least!

Mar 2, 2013 12:11 AM

"@MGIFINC: @realDonaldTrump --- Call Rosie O'Donnell to help you."She can't help herself - she's sad, angry and pathetic!

Jul 13, 2013 6:02 PM

Rosie O'Donnell just said she felt "shame" at being fat-not politically correct! She killed Star Jones for weight loss surgery, just had it!

May 9, 2014 7:22 PM

Rosie is crude, rude, obnoxious and dumb - other than that I like her very much!

Jul 11, 2014 6:07 AM

No surprise. @Rosie is failing on @TheView.Terrible ratings."Malcontent" & another season is "out of the question" http://t.co/RAh59q06N4

Dec 1, 2014 5:02 PM

I predicted Rosie O'Donnell would fail at the View, and was right. Now I predict Rosie will take over for Brian Williams!

Feb 7, 2015 7:10 PM

"@taylor70778592: #ObamaLovesAmerica like Rosie O'Donnell loves Donald Trump" Interesting.

Feb 21, 2015 7:25 PM

"@StefanVersac: @megynkelly @ChrisStirewalt @ChrisChristie @realDonaldTrump Rosie O'Donnell was the best answer of that whole debate"

AUG 7, 2015 4:05 AM

It was Rosie O'Donnell who ate the cake in the vicious Hillary commercial about me, not Crooked Hillary! @marthamaccallum

MAY 10, 2016 8:57 AM

Megyn Kelly

Wow, @megynkelly really bombed tonight. People are going wild on twitter! Funny to watch.

AUG 7, 2015 12:40 AM

.@megynkelly must have had a terrible vacation, she is really off her game. Was afraid to confront Dr. Cornel West. No clue on immigration!

AUG 24, 2015 8:42 PM

Do you ever notice that lightweight @megynkelly constantly goes after me but when I hit back it is totally sexist. She is highly overrated!

SEP 22, 2015 7:00 PM

Megyn Kelly has two really dumb puppets, Chris Stirewalt & Marc Threaten (a Bushy) who do exactly what she says. All polls say I won debates

OCT 15, 2015 9:00 PM

Isn't it terrible that @megynkelly used a poll not used before (I.B.D.) when I was down, but refuses to use it now when I am up?

NOV 4, 2015 8:28 AM

I won every debate so far according to all debate polls including @DRUDGE_REPORT, @TIME @Slate and more. Too bad dopey @megynkelly lies!

DEC 15, 2015 9:23 AM

.@megynkelly, the most overrated anchor at @FoxNews, worked hard to explain away the new Monmouth poll 41 to 14 or 27 pt lead. She said 15!

DEC 15, 2015 7:30 AM

.@megynkelly is very bad at math. She was totally unable to figure out the difference between me and Cruz in the new Monmouth Poll 41to14.

DEC 15, 2015 7:34 AM

.@megynkelly recently said that she can't be wooed by Trump. She is so average in every way, who the hell wants to woo her!

JAN 11, 2016 12:20 PM

Based on @MegynKelly's conflict of interest and bias she should not be allowed to be a moderator of the next debate.

JAN 23, 2016 8:52 AM

I refuse to call Megyn Kelly a bimbo, because that would not be politically correct. Instead I will only call her a lightweight reporter!

JAN 27, 2016 3:44 AM

Why does @megynkelly devote so much time on her shows to me, almost always negative? Without me her ratings would tank. Get a life Megyn!

FEB 16, 2016 7:58 PM

Can't watch Crazy Megyn anymore. Talks about me at 43% but never mentions that there are four people in race. With two people, big & over!

MAR 15, 2016 5:05 PM

Watching other networks and local news. Really good night! Crazy @megynkelly is unwatchable.

MAR 15, 2016 5:09 PM

Everybody should boycott the @megynkelly show. Never worth watching. Always a hit on Trump! She is sick, & the most overrated person on tv.

MAR 18, 2016 2:55 PM

If crazy @megynkelly didn't cover me so much on her terrible show, her ratings would totally tank. She is so average in so many ways!

MAR 19, 2016 10:16 AM

Is it possible for @megynkelly to cover anyone but Donald Trump - almost her whole shoe, every night - and she so misrepresents my positions

DELETED AFTER 33 SECONDS AT 9:40 PM ON APR 1, 2016

Is it possible for @megynkelly to cover anyone but Donald Trump on her terrible show. She totally misrepresents my words and positions! BAD.

APR 1, 2016 8:44 PM

So the highly overrated anchor, @megynkelly, is allowed to constantly say bad things about me on her show, but I can't fight back? Wrong!

MAR 20, 2016 12:10 PM

Highly overrated & crazy @megynkelly is always complaining about Trump and yet she devotes her shows to me. Focus on others Megyn!

MAR 17, 2016 9:58 AM

Katie Couric

Katie Couric, the third rate reporter, who has been largely forgotten, should be ashamed of herself for the fraudulent editing of her doc.

MAY 31, 2016 4:14 PM

CHAPTER 12

On the Campaign Trail— Crooked Hillary, Lyin' Ted, and Little Marco

I am getting bad marks from certain pundits because.I have a small campaign staff. But small is good, flexible, save money and number one!

DELETED AFTER 1 HOUR AT 9:51 AM ON JUN 6, 2016

This has been a very difficult decision regarding the Presidential run and I want to thank all my twitter fans for your fantastic support.

MAY 16, 2011 2:47 PM

Thank you for your support my candidacy! #MAGA #ImWithYou https://t.co/dRCbTCCifs

DELETED AFTER 2 MINUTES AT 8:54 AM ON AUG 7, 2016

Here are his tweets against opponents, retweets from supporters, and announcements leading up to Election Day.

Every poll done on debate last night, from Drudge to News-max to Time Magazine, had me winning in a landslide. #MakeAmericaGreatAgain!

SEP 17, 2015 12:18 PM

After the way I beat Gov. Scott Walker (and Jeb, Rand, Marco and all others) in the Presidential Primaries, no way he would ever endorse me!

MAR 28, 2016 6:13 PM

"Little Marco"

I laugh when I see Marco Rubio and Jeb Bush pretending to "love" each other, with each talking of their great friendship. Typical phony pols

MAY 17, 2015 6:54 PM

Further proof that Gang of Eight member Marco Rubio is weak on illegal immigration is Paul Singer's, Mr. Amnesty, endorsement.Rubs can't win

NOV 1, 2015 7:29 AM

.@JRubinBlogger one of the dumber bloggers @washingtonpost only writes purposely inaccurate pieces on me. She is in love with Marco Rubio?

DEC 4, 2015 3:37 PM

"@mitchellvii: My prediction on the Trey Gowdy endorsement of Rubio is that it will do nothing for Rubio and finish Gowdy."

DEC 27, 2015 7:45 AM

"@Sir_Max: andreajmarkley: Rubio finally gets an endorsement – from #Benghazi loser Gowdy #Tcot #pjnet https://t.co/lJcHG0I-HaM via dailyne

DEC 27, 2015 7:37 AM

Lightweight Marco Rubio was working hard last night. The problem is, he is a choker, and once a choker, always a chocker! Mr. Meltdown.

DELETED AFTER 4 HOURS AT 11:50 AM ON FEB 26, 2016

Leightweight chocker Marco Rubio looks like a little boy on stage. Not presidential material!

DELETED AFTER 1 HOUR AT 11:17 AM ON FEB 26, 2016

While I hear the Koch brothers are in big financial trouble (oil), word is they have chosen little Marco Rubio, the lightweight from Florida

FEB 28, 2016 6:28 AM

Little Marco Rubio, the lightweight no show Senator from Florida, is set to be the "puppet" of the special interest Koch brothers. WATCH!

FEB 28, 2016 11:07 AM

Little Marco Rubio, the lightweight no show Senator from Florida is just another Washington politician. https://t.co/NsLrHrqjdx

FEB 28, 2016 12:50 PM

Little Marco Rubio is just another Washington D.C. politician that is all talk and no action. #RobotRubio https://t.co/HJWJeoZn4o

FEB 28, 2016 1:45 PM

Little Marco Rubio gave amnesty to criminal aliens guilty of "sex offenses." DISGRACE! https://t.co/mZwpynzsLb

FEB 28, 2016 2:06 PM

Little Marco Rubio treated America's ICE officers "like absolute trash" in order to pass Obama's amnesty. https://t.co/gm2wurLjFz

FEB 28, 2016 2:19 PM

Word is-early voting in FL is very dishonest. Little Marco, his State Chairman, & their minions are working overtime-trying to rig the vote.

MAR 12, 2016 1:06 PM

We are asking law enforcement to check for dishonest early voting in Florida- on behalf of little Marco Rubio. No way to run a country!

MAR 12, 2016 1:07 PM

Carly Fiorina

Carly Fiorina is terrible at business--the last thing our country needs! http://t.co/n7lO0llhK8

SEP 21, 2015 9:56 AM

Gov. George Pataki of New York

.@GovernorPataki was a terrible governor of NY, one of the worst -- would've been swamped if he ran again!

JUL 1, 2015 4:09 PM

.@GovernorPataki did a terrible job as Governor of New York. If he ran again, he would have lost in a landslide. He and Graham ZERO in polls

AUG 25, 2015 7:49 AM

Why is someone like George Pataki, who did a terrible job as Governor of N.Y. and registers ZERO in the polls, allowed on the debate stage?

SEP 13, 2015 8:41 AM

"@twlhb: @realDonaldTrump @GovernorPataki just called you "this PRESIDENT" !!! https://t.co/z5pRWZgS08" But I don't want his endorsement!

DEC 15, 2015 7:01 PM

Hillary Investigation

"@FoxNews: .@JamesRosenFNC: "Never before has a president endorsed someone under investigation by @TheJusticeDept." https://t.co/fX5bs8fzac

JUN 10, 2016 7:20 AM

What He Will/Won't Endorse—Policies

.@thehill Your story about me & the carbon tax is absolutely incorrect—it is just the opposite. I will not support or endorse a carbon tax!

MAY 13, 2016 1:40 PM

Violent crime is rising across the United States, yet the DNC convention ignored it. Crime reduction will be one of my top priorities.

JUL 30, 2016 1:06 PM

Ford is MOVING jobs from Michigan to Mexico AGAIN! http://t.co/TgVQ1458AJ As President, this will stop on Day One! Jobs will stay here.

JUL 14, 2015 7:55 AM

"Lyin'" Ted Cruz

Wacko @glennbeck is a sad answer to the @SarahPalinUSA endorsement that Cruz so desperately wanted. Glenn is a failing, crying, lost soul!

JAN 21, 2016 8:42 AM

Amazing that Ted Cruz can't even get a Senator like @BenSasse, who is easy, to endorse him. Not one Senator is endorsing Canada Ted!

JAN 29, 2016 8:25 PM

.@bobvanderplaats is a total phony and con man. When I wouldn't give him free hotel rooms and much more, he endorsed Cruz. @foxandfriends

JAN 31, 2016 7:42 AM

.@bobvanderplaats is a total phony and dishonest guy. Asked me for expensive hotel rooms, free (and more). I said pay and he endorsed Cruz!

JAN 31, 2016 7:31 AM

Hey @glennbeck- see how I beat your boy Ted- in your own Blaze poll? Your endorsement means nothing! #GOPDebate

FEB 14, 2016 1:26 AM

Have a good chance to win Texas on Tuesday. Cruz is a nasty guy, not one Senate endorsement and, despite talk, gets nothing done. Loser!

FEB 26, 2016 9:02 AM

Lyin' Ted Cruz lost all five races on Tuesday-and he was just given the jinx - a Lindsey Graham endorsement. Also backed Jeb. Lindsey got 0!

MAR 18, 2016 11:42 AM

@LindseyGrahamSC made horrible statements about @SenTedCruz – and then he endorsed him. No wonder nobody trusts politicians!

MAR 18, 2016 2:03 PM

I think having Jeb's endorsement hurts Lyin' Ted. Jeb spent more than $150,000,000 and got nothing. I spent a fraction of that and am first!

MAR 23, 2016 03:02 PM

Jeb Bush

Everybody is laughing at Jeb Bush-spent $100 million and is at bottom of pack. A pathetic figure!

FEB 8, 2016 8:38 AM

Just watched Jeb's ad where he desperately needed mommy to help him. Jeb --- mom can't help you with ISIS, the Chinese or with Putin.

JAN 22, 2016 8:02 PM

The arrogant young woman who questioned me in such a nasty fashion at No Labels yesterday was a Jeb staffer! HOW CAN HE BEAT RUSSIA & CHINA?

OCT 13, 2015 6:39 AM

How can Jeb Bush expect to deal with China, Russia + Iran if he gets caught doing a "plant" during my speech yesterday in NH?

OCT 13, 2015 10:52 AM

.@JebBush's opening and closing in the debate were said by all to be terrible--fumbled around, incoherent.

DEC 22, 2015 4:25 PM

.@JebBush was terrible on Face The Nation today. Being at 2% and falling seems to have totally affected his confidence. A basket case!

DEC 20, 2015 6:13 PM

The last thing our country needs is another BUSH! Dumb as a rock!

DEC 18, 2015 3:59 PM

Just out Nevada poll shows Jeb Bush at 1%, he should take his dumb mouthpiece, @LindseyGrahamSC, and just go home.

FEB 17, 2016 11:10 AM

.@JebBush today said he didn't want to be the front-runner, he would rather be where he is now, 2%. That is the talk of a loser, can't win!

DEC 20, 2015 11:42 PM

Sen. Lindsey Graham embarrassed himself with his failed run for President and now further embarrasses himself with endorsement of Bush.

JAN 15, 2016 10:30 AM

Jeb Bush, who did poorly last night in the debate and whose chances of winning are zero, just got Graham endorsement. Graham quit at 0.

JAN 15, 2016 10:17 AM

Low energy Jeb Bush just endorsed a man he truly hates, Lyin' Ted Cruz. Honestly, I can't blame Jeb in that I drove him into oblivion!

MAR 23, 2016 2:49 PM

CHAPTER 13

Conventions and
the Campaign Trail

Conventions

Here's a sneak peek at the @DNC convention theme: "It's not our fault. Blame Bush. Oh, and government built it."

AUG 23, 2012 8:31 AM

I am sure the @NCGOP will do a great job bracketing the @DNC convention. They are a tremendous statewide organization.

AUG 24, 2012 3:16 PM

Florida has been very good to me. I am really esxcited to give back at the Sarasota GOP event and @RNC convention. Will be fun!

AUG 24, 2012 2:24 PM

A hurricane will be coming to Tampa. My @RNC convention surprise hits Monday night!

AUG 24, 2012 7:55 AM

My @FoxNews @TeamCavuto interview discussing the @RNC Convention, businesses making products in China and unemployment http://t.co/JhuoyBU8

Aug 28, 2012 12:55 PM

Thank you to all of the television viewers that made my speech at the Republican National Convention #1 over Crooked Hillary and DEMS.

Jul 30, 2016 6:00 PM

The dishonest media is fawning over the Democratic Convention. I wonder why, then, my speech had millions of more viewers than Crooked H

Jul 31, 2016 3:09 PM

During the GOP convention, CNN cut away from the victims of illegal immigrant violence. They don't want them heard.

Aug 1, 2016 5:54 PM

The media coverage this morning of the very average Clinton speech and Convention is a joke. @CNN and the little watched @Morning_Joe = SAD!

Jul 29, 2016 7:40 AM

Not one American flag on the massive stage at the Democratic National Convention until people started complaining-then a small one. Pathetic

Jul 27, 2016 8:01 AM

The Democratic Convention has paid ZERO respect to the great police and law enforcement professionals of our country. No recognition - SAD!

Jul 27, 2016 4:50 AM

I hate to say it, but the Republican Convention was far more interesting (with a much more beautiful set) than the Democratic Convention!

JUL 26, 2016 9:08 PM

Why aren't the Democrats speaking about ISIS, bad trade deals, broken borders, police and law and order. The Republican Convention was great

JUL 26, 2016 7:38 AM

Wow, the Republican Convention went so smoothly compared to the Dems total mess. But fear not, the dishonest media will find a good spinnnn!

JUL 25, 2016 8:47 AM

The ratings for the Republican National Convention were very good, but for the final night, my speech, great. Thank you!

JUL 24, 2016 6:47 PM

If the Republican Convention had blown up with e-mails, resignation of boss and the beat down of a big player. (Bernie), media would go wild

JUL 24, 2016 4:53 PM

I always said that Debbie Wasserman Schultz was overrated. The Dems Convention is cracking up and Bernie is exhausted, no energy left!

JUL 24, 2016 3:30 PM

Funny that the Democrats would have their convention in Pennsylvania where her husband and her killed so many jobs. I will bring jobs back!

JUL 23, 2016 10:01 AM

One of the best produced, including the incredible stage & set, in the history of conventions. Great unity! Big T.V. ratings! @KarlRove

JUL 22, 2016 9:06 AM

Our next Vice President of the United States of America, Gov. @Mike_Pence! #GOPinCLE   #GOPConvention#AmericaFirst https://t.co/TZT3XcKp1c

JUL 20, 2016 10:49 PM

Watching the #GOPConvention #AmericaFirst #RNCinCLE

JUL 20, 2016 6:49 PM

The ROLL CALL is beginning at the Republican National Convention. Very exciting!

JUL 19, 2016 5:12 PM

It was truly an honor to introduce my wife, Melania. Her speech and demeanor were absolutely incredible. Very proud! #GOPConvention

JUL 18, 2016 11:14 PM

Will be on @OreillyFactor tonight at 8:30pm @FoxNews- prior to Melania's speech at the #GOPConvention. Tune in- she will do great! #RNCinCLE

JUL 18, 2016 7:21 PM

#MakeAmericaSafeAgain! #GOPConvention #RNCinCLE https://t.co/QniZIsGrG8 https://t.co/Kvq6r6WkQ1

JUL 18, 2016 6:04 PM

Looking forward to being at the convention tonight to watch all of the wonderful speakers including my wife, Melania. Place looks beautiful!

JUL 18, 2016 12:28 PM

Convention speaker schedule to be released tomorrow. Let today be devoted to Crooked Hillary and the rigged system under which we live.

JUL 6, 2016 10:32 AM

Hillary Clinton should ask why the Democrat pols in Atlantic City made all the wrong moves - ConventionCenter, Airport - and destroyed City

JUL 6, 2016 8:12 AM

The speakers slots at the Republican Convention are totally filled, with a long waiting list of those that want to speak - Wednesday release

JUL 2, 2016 6:55 AM

Iron Mike Tyson was not asked to speak at the Convention though I'm sure he would do a good job if he was. The media makes everything up!

JUN 28, 2016 9:55 PM

The convention in Cleveland will be amazing! https://t.co/NlF2Gcr915

JUN 17, 2016 6:55 PM

Join me on Wednesday, May 25th at the Anaheim Convention Center! #Trump2016 #MAGA Tickets: https://t.co/mmPck1HYrC https://t.co/xGkVbxTamz

MAY 22, 2016 2:46 PM

Colorado Trump Delegates Scratched from Ballots at GOP Convention https://t.co/WLkmYjJJR9

APR 11, 2016 3:40 PM

"@vivhall3: @realDonaldTrump here your delegate replaced at CO GOP convention. https://t.co/NxYhzdcMS0" Very sad!

APR 9, 2016 9:44 PM

Will be at Fort Worth (Texas) Convention Center at 11:30 A.M. Big crowd - get there early! Big announcement to be made!

FEB 26, 2016 11:07 AM

Wow! Honored to be chosen by the highly respected + accurate Washington & Lee Mock Convention. I hope you are right - I will make you proud!

FEB 13, 2016 7:00 PM

Phoenix Convention Center officials did not want to have thousands of people standing outside in the heat, so they let them in. A GREAT day!

JUL 12, 2015 8:21 AM

Convention Center officials in Phoenix don't want to admit that they broke the fire code by allowing 12-15,000 people in 4,000 code room.

JUL 12, 2015 8:18 AM

Laura--Massive crowd, had to move to Phoenix Convention Center. https://t.co/76fQCecDBd

JUL 10, 2015 1:21 PM

Loved doing #NCGOPConvention keynote speech last night! Unbelievable reception. Had the biggest crowds by far of any of the GOP candidates.

JUN 7, 2015 4:08 PM

Excited to be returning to the @NCGOP State Convention as the Keynote of Saturday's dinner! @NCGOP is a strong Conservative state party!

JUN 3, 2015 2:28 PM

Looking forward to speaking @nranews Convention in Nashville http://t.co/Y6VYva0Gn8 The 2nd Amendment is a right, not a privilege!

MAR 26, 2015 1:58 PM

ICYMI, my speech this past Monday at the South Carolina Tea Party Convention in Myrtle Beach http://t.co/2OlmwXgruv #SCTeaParty15

JAN 21, 2015 12:22 PM

Via @BPolitics by @Griffin "Aboard Donald Trump's 757 at the South Carolina Tea Party Convention" https://t.co/fSb6yvEqUY

JAN 19, 2015 10:42 PM

"TEA TALK: Highlights from Monday convention speech from Donald Trump" http://t.co/HbeF6TD2A8 via @myrbeachonline by @TSN_MPrabhu

JAN 19, 2015 10:32 PM

"Trump arrives for SC Tea Party Convention in Myrtle Beach" http://t.co/Gg0Evnb5FR via @WCBD

JAN 19, 2015 8:57 PM

Via @CarolinaLive by @JoelAllenWPDE: "Big names wrap up largest ever SC Tea Party Coalition Convention" http://t.co/52xCeywzZp

JAN 19, 2015 7:37 PM

Via @myrbeachonline by @TSN_MPrabhu: "Donald Trump states case for becoming POTUS at SC Tea Party convention" http://t.co/b3HWGXEkXu

JAN 19, 2015 6:58 PM

"Donald Trump to headline SC Tea Party Convention" http://t.co/0ja1yS3gXO via @wyffnews4

JAN 17, 2015 7:53 PM

Via @WTOC11: "Donald Trump headlines Tea Party Convention in Myrtle Beach" http://t.co/kTuSn6eSEs Looking forward to visiting SC on Monday!

JAN 16, 2015 11:56 AM

Looking forward to keynoting the South Carolina Tea Party Convention in Myrtle Beach on Monday at 3:20PM! http://t.co/qkMriOTcWb

JAN 14, 2015 3:40 PM

Via @wbtwnews13 by @elizabethk_wbtw: "Donald Trump will deliver keynote address to the SC Tea Party Convention" http://t.co/QHAkXuH8CC

JAN 9, 2015 5:37 PM

Via @thestate by @andyshain: "Donald Trump joins other 2016 prospects speaking at SC Tea Party Convention" http://t.co/cMriNEirEU

JAN 7, 2015 6:19 PM

Via @BreitbartNews by @mboyle1: "Exclusive: Trump To Address South Carolina Tea Party Convention" http://t.co/Jtut7sRCNX

JAN 7, 2015 2:53:PM

It is so sad to see what has happened to Atlantic City. So many bad decisions by the pols over the years - airport, convention center, etc.

SEP 16, 2014 7:16 AM

"@LaydeePrivatier: @realDonaldTrump I enjoyed your speech at the Republican Convention in New Hampshire immensely!" Thank you!

APR 18, 2014 6:14 AM

Looking forward to speaking @acnnews International Convention tomorrow morning in Charlotte, NC http://t.co/hhlUeV5M

FEB 15, 2013 3:09 PM

Of the 9 battleground states, we only carried North Carolina. I'm proud of @NCGOP & glad I delivered keynote at their state convention.

NOV 9, 2012 10:23 AM

Glad to hear North Carolina is solid for @MittRomney. It started trending for Mitt solidly after my speech at the @NCGOP
convention.

OCT 24, 2012 4:55 PM

.@MittRomney's @RNC convention came in over $3M under
budget. Barack's @DNC convention is over $10M in debt. What
a surprise!

OCT 19, 2012 3:30 PM

This morning @nbc @todayshow played some of the @RNC video I
filmed for the Tampa Conventionhttp://t.co/ogglpBfQ

SEP 18, 2012 2:18 PM

Obama's convention bounce is gone. @MittRomney has retaken the
lead in the latest @RasmussenPoll http://t.co/yOw3U3ja

SEP 13, 2012 1:32 PM

Dems had a very good and professional convention. The Republicans must be smart and tough--and fast!

SEP 7, 2012 10:00 AM

The delegates at the @DNC convention keep shouting "Four More
Years." Four more years of 18% real unemployment and another
$6T in debt?

SEP 6, 2012 12:59 PM

Political strategist Stuart Stevens,who led Romney down the tubes in
what should have been an easy victory,has terrible political instincts!

OCT 5, 2015 6:40 PM

John Kerry

I wonder if when Secy. Kerry goes to Iraq and Afghanistan he pushes
hard for them to look at GLOBAL WARMING and study the carbon footprint?

JUN 23, 2014 11:26 AM

Re Kerry admitting to "working" for Pastor Abedini's release--why has US already released Iranian spies & nuclear scientist? Dumb!

Dec 10, 2013 5:00 PM

Tim Kaine

Why did Tim Kaine have no problem when he took far more money as Governor of Virginia than Bob McDonald. Crooked Hillary & rigged system!

Deleted after 55 minutes at 8:30 PM on Jul 23, 2016

John Lewis

Congressman John Lewis should finally focus on the burning and crime infested inner-cities of the U.S. I can use all the help I can get!

Jan 14, 2017 7:22 PM

Glenn Beck

Word is that crying @GlennBeck left the GOP and doesn't have the right to vote in the Republican primary. Dumb as a rock.

Jan 23, 2016 8:21 PM

Wacky @glennbeck who always seems to be crying (worse than Boehner) speaks badly of me only because I refuse to do his show--a real nut job!

Oct 8, 2015 8:44 AM

I hear @glennbeck is in big trouble. Unlike me, his viewers & ratings are way down & he has become irrelevant—glad I didn't do his show.

Oct 8, 2015 8:45 AM

Failing host @glennbeck, a mental basketcase, loves SUPERPACS - in other words, he wants your politicians totally controlled by lobbyists!

Oct 29, 2015 8:42 AM

.@GlennBeck got fired like a dog by #Fox. The Blaze is failing and he wanted to have me on his show. I said no - because he is irrelevant.

Dec 16, 2015 8:09 PM

Wacko @glennbeck is a sad answer to the @SarahPalinUSA endorsement that Cruz so desperately wanted. Glenn is a failing, crying, lost soul!

JAN 21, 2016 5:42 AM

The only reason irrelevant @GlennBeck doesn't like me is I refused to do his failing show - asked many times. Very few listeners - sad!

JAN 22, 2016 5:33 PM

Ted Cruz

Have a good chance to win Texas on Tuesday. Cruz is a nasty guy, not one Senate endorsement and, despite talk, gets nothing done. Loser!

FEB 26, 2016 9:02 AM

Wow @SenTedCruz, that is some low level ad you did using a picture Melania in a G.Q. shoot.Be careful or I will spill the beans on your wife

DELETED AFTER 26 SECONDS AT 1:26 AM ON MAR 23, 2016

Lying Ted Cruz and leightweight chocker Marco Rubio teamed up last night in a last ditch effort to stop our great movement. They failed!

DELETED AFTER 1 HOUR AT 11:16 AM ON FEB 26, 2016

Ted Cruz didn't win Iowa, he illegally stole it. That is why all of the polls were so wrong any why he got more votes than anticipated. Bad!

DELETED AFTER 1 MINUTE AT 8:41 AM ON FEB 3, 2016

Lyin' Ted Cruz, who can never beat Hilary Clinton, has chosen a running mate who was unable to catch on in her own failed campaign. No path!

DELETED AFTER 27 SECONDS AT 7:25 AM ON APR 28, 2016

Can you believe that Ted Cruz, who has been killing our country on trade for so long, just put out a Wisconsin ad talking about trade?

DELETED AFTER 2 MINUTES AT 5:50 PM ON APR 1, 2016

I have millions more votes hundreds more dels than Cruz or Kasich and yet am not being treated properly by the Republican Party or the RNC.

DELETED AFTER 8 MINUTES AT 10:19 AM ON MAR 29, 2016

Wow, the ridiculous deal made between Lyin'Ted Cruz and 1 for 42 John Kasich has just blown up. What a dumb deal - dead on arrival!

APR 29, 2016 6:22 AM

The Cruz-Kasich pact is under great strain. This joke of a deal is falling apart, not being honored and almost dead. Very dumb!

APR 26, 2016 5:42 AM

Justice Ruth Bader Ginsburg

Justice Ginsburg of the U.S. Supreme Court has embarrassed all by making very dumb political statements about me. Her mind is shot - resign!

JUL 12, 2016 11:54 PM

Greta Van Susteren

Why does @Greta have a fired Bushy like dummy, John Sununu on- spewing false info? I will beat Hillary by a lot, she wants no part of Trump.

JAN 21, 2016 7:54 PM

I'll be discussing a variety of topics tonight with Greta Van Susteren, 10 p.m. on Fox News. It will be the first of a two part series.

NOV 3, 2010 4:11 PM

Crooked Hillary

Crooked Hillary Clinton looks presidential? I don't think so! Four more years of Obama and our country will never come back. ISIS LAUGHS!

MAY 20, 2016 3:08 AM

Watched Crooked Hillary Clinton and Tim Kaine on 60 Minutes. No way they are going to fix America's problems. ISIS & all others laughing!

JUL 24, 2016 4:59 PM

If Crooked Hillary Clinton can't close the deal on Crazy Bernie, how is she going to take on China, Russia, ISIS and all of the others?

MAY 13, 2016 8:03 PM

If Russia or any other country or person has Hillary Clinton's 33,000 illegally deleted emails, perhaps they should share them with the FBI!

JUL 27, 2016 11:16 AM

The new joke in town is that Russia leaked the disastrous DNC e-mails, which should never have been written (stupid), because Putin likes me

JUL 25, 2016 6:31 AM

Black Lives Matter protesters totally disrupt Hillary Clinton event. She looked lost. This is not what we need with ISIS, CHINA, RUSSIA etc.

OCT 31, 2015 6:27 AM

The attack on Mosul is turning out to be a total disaster. We gave them months of notice. U.S. is looking so dumb. VOTE TRUMP and WIN AGAIN!

OCT 23, 2016 6:40 PM

"@LouDobbs: Hillary Just Handed @realDonaldTrump a Huge Gift: Promising to Put Bubba in Charge of the Economy! #MakeAmericaGreatAgain!

MAY 17, 2016 9:41 PM

@TomOdell: .@FoxNews - Pope who lives in a Vatican city fortified with huge walls thinks it's wrong to build walls? Really? https://t.co... =

FEB 18, 2016 2:42 PM RT

Huge crowd expected tomorrow night! VT Police say first come, first serve. Arrive early!

JAN 6, 2016 3:22 PM

«@djw11223: @realDonaldTrump The crowd was HUGE #MakeAmericaGreatAgain https://t.co/xKq957P6yr"

JAN 4, 2016 10:36 PM

Hillary says "take back Mosul?" We would have NEVER lost Mosul- if it wasn't for #CrookedHillary. #DrainTheSwamp

OCT 19, 2016 9:14 PM

The so-called Commission on Presidential Debates admitted to us that the DJT audio & sound level was very bad. So why didn't they fix it?

OCT 1, 2016 3:47 PM

Russia took Crimea during the so-called Obama years. Who wouldn't know this and why does Obama get a free pass?

SEP 13, 2016 10:21 PM

A detainee released from Gitmo has killed an American. When will our so-called "leaders" ever learn!

MAR 28, 2016 12:25 PM

Hillary said with respect to ISIS, "we are finally where we need to be." Do we want 4 more years of incompetent leadership? MAGA!

DEC 21, 2015 7:34 AM

The people of South Carolina are embarrassed by Nikki Hailey!

DELETED AFTER 18 MINUTES AT 2:43 PM ON MAR 1, 2016

@CLewandowski_: Gov Nikki Haley just became a liability for Rubio after this was published to social media!

MAR 1, 2016 2:14 PM RT

Khizr Khan (Gold Star Father of Iraqi Soldier)

I was viciously attacked by Mr. Khan at the Democratic Convention. Am I not allowed to respond? Hillary voted for the Iraq war, not me!

JUL 31, 2016 9:32 AM

Mr. Khan, who does not know me, viciously attacked me from the stage of the DNC and is now all over T.V. doing the same - Nice!

AUG 1, 2016 6:10 AM

This story is not about Mr. Khan, who is all over the place doing interviews, but rather RADICAL ISLAMIC TERRORISM and the U.S. Get smart!

AUG 1, 2016 6:27 AM

Tony Schwartz

I havn't seen @tonyschwartz in many years, he hardly knows me. Never liked his style. Super lib, Crooked H supporter. Irrelevant dope!

SEP 9, 2016 10:57 PM

Dummy writer @tonyschwartz, who wanted to do a second book with me for years (I said no), is now a hostile basket case who feels jilted!

SEP 9, 2016 10:47 PM

Ron Fournier: "Clinton Used Secret Server To Protect #CircleOfEnrichment"

OCT 27, 2016 9:10 AM

Mexico

Mexico will pay for the wall!

SEP 1, 2016 5:31 AM

Mexico will pay for the wall - 100%! #MakeAmericaGreatAgain #ImWithYou

Aug 31, 2016 11:58 PM

Great trip to Mexico today - wonderful leadership and high quality people! Look forward to our next meeting

Aug 31, 2016 7:43 PM

Hillary Clinton didn't go to Louisiana, and now she didn't go to Mexico. She doesn't have the drive or stamina to MAKE AMERICA GREAT AGAIN!

Aug 31, 2016 7:40 PM

Former President Vicente Fox, who is railing against my visit to Mexico today, also invited me when he apologized for using the "f bomb."

Aug 31, 2016 8:07 AM

I have accepted the invitation of President Enrique Pena Nieto, of Mexico, and look very much forward to meeting him tomorrow.

Aug 30, 2016 9:33 PM

Vast numbers of manufacturing jobs in Pennsylvania have moved to Mexico and other countries. That will end when I win!

Aug 1, 2016 8:33 PM

The "Rust Belt" was created by politicians like the Clintons who allowed our jobs to be stolen from us by other countries like Mexico. END!

Jul 30, 2016 5:12 PM

McAllen, Texas- 8 miles from U.S. - Mexico border. #Trump2016 Video: https://t.co/pQ4nSTnVrK https://t.co/dKBTP1QjH3

Jun 16, 2016 11:50 AM

The protesters in New Mexico were thugs who were flying the Mexican flag. The rally inside was big and beautiful, but outside, criminals!

MAY 25, 2016 8:39 AM

Crooked Hillary just can't close the deal with Bernie. It will be the same way with ISIS, and China on trade, and Mexico at the border. Bad!

MAY 8, 2016 3:15 PM

We must build a great wall between Mexico and the United States! https://t.co/05SjuRJFbf

APR 1, 2016 4:49 PM

Ohio is losing jobs to Mexico, now losing Ford (and many others). Kasich is weak on illegal immigration. We need strong borders now!

MAR 15, 2016 10:03 AM

North Carolina lost 300,000 manufacturing jobs and Ohio lost 400,000 since 2000. Going to Mexico etc. NO MORE IF I WIN, WE WILL BRING BACK!

MAR 15, 2016 8:37 AM

Absentee Governor Kasich voted for NAFTA and NAFTA devastated Ohio - a disaster from which it never recovered. Kasich is good for Mexico!

MAR 12, 2016 8:35 AM

Great POLL numbers are coming out all over. People don't want another four years of Obama, and Crooked Hillary would be even worse. #MAGA

JUL 25, 2016 9:05 AM

FMR PRES of Mexico, Vicente Fox horribly used the F word when discussing the wall. He must apologize! If I did that there would be a uproar!

FEB 25, 2016 3:27 PM

"@AmFree: #Trump On #Ford, #Carrier, Shipping #Jobs To #Mexico: 'I'm The Only One Who Understands What's Going On' https://t.co/JsuiHpQpXX"

FEB 13, 2016 2:24 PM

Now an additional 600-700 jobs in America (2,000) being eliminated for move to Mexico- via Hartford Courant. https://t.co/bOIYQLqGRG

FEB 13, 2016 10:16 AM

.@AnnCoulter has been amazing. We will win and establish strong borders, we will build a WALL and Mexicowill pay. We will be great again!

JAN 23, 2016 9:45 AM

Third Debate

She'll say anything and change NOTHING! #MAGA #BigLeagueTruth https://t.co/6E767Uw6Dj

OCT 19, 2016 8:58 PM

One of my first acts as President will be to deport the drug lords and then secure the border. #Debate #MAGA

OCT 19, 2016 08:23 PM

Hindsight

Just announced that Iraq (U.S.) is preparing for battle to reclaim Mosul. Why do they have to announce this? Makes mission much harder!

OCT 2, 2016 6:45 PM

Trump called Russia ahead of dropping Tomahawk missiles on a Syrian air base in April 2017.

John Kasich

Ohio Gov. Kasich voted for NAFTA from which Ohio has never recovered. Now he want TPP, which will be even worse. Ohio steel & coal dying!

DELETED AFTER 25 MINUTES AT 7:59 AM ON MAR 13, 2016

Governor John Kasich of the GREAT, GREAT, GREAT State of Ohio called to congratulate me on the win. The people of Ohio were incredible!

NOV 13, 2016 10:28 AM

John Kasich was never asked by me to be V.P. Just arrived in Cleveland - will be a great two days!

JUL 20, 2016 1:48 PM

Joe Scarborough initially endorsed Jeb Bush and Jeb crashed, then John Kasich and that didn't work. Not much power or insight!

MAY 6, 2016 1:03 PM

Wow, the ridiculous deal made between Lyin'Ted Cruz and 1 for 42 John Kasich has just blown up. What a dumb deal - dead on arrival!

APR 29, 2016 6:22 AM

As soon as John Kasich is hit with negative ads, he will drop like a rock in the polls against Crooked Hillary Clinton. I will win!

APR 23, 2016 8:48 PM

Both Ted Cruz and John Kasich have no path to victory. They should both drop out of the race so that the Republican Party can unify!

APR 21, 2016 4:47 PM

Failed Presidential Candidate Mitt Romney was campaigning with John Kasich & Marco Rubio, and now he is endorsing Ted Cruz. 1/2

MAR 18, 2016 3:21 PM

In presidential voting so far, John Kasich is ZERO for 22. So why would he be a good candidate? Hillary would beat him, I will beat Hillary!

Mar 15, 2016 11:03 AM

Watching John Kasich being interviewed - acting so innocent and like such a nice guy. Remember him in second debate, until I put him down.

Mar 15, 2016 9:53 AM

Do the people of Ohio know that John Kasich is STRONGLY in favor of Common Core! In other words, education of your children from D.C. No way

Mar 12, 2016 5:47 PM

"@Barber2012Jeff: @realDonaldTrump John Kasich-it didn't work I'm still voting for #Trump" John has done so poorly in the debates he's done!

Nov 29, 2015 9:57 PM

John Kasich was managing director of Lehman Brothers when it crashed, bringing down the world and ruining people's lives. A total failure!

Nov 19, 2015 8:55 PM

Once John Kasich announced he was running for president, and opened his mouth, people realized he was a complete & total dud!

Nov 19, 2015 8:47 PM

John Kasich fell right into President Obama's trap on ObamaCare, and the people of Ohio are suffering for it. Shame!

Nov 19, 2015 8:06 PM

I loved beating John Kasich in the debates, but it was easy—he came in dead last!

Nov 19, 2015 8:06 PM

I want to do negative ads on John Kasich, but he is so irrelevant to the race that I don't want to waste my money.

Nov 19, 2015 8:05 PM

John Kasich, despite being Governor of Ohio, is losing to me in the Ohio polls. Pathetic!

Nov 19, 2015 8:05 PM

John Kasich should focus his special interest money on building up his failed image, not negative ads on me.

Nov 19, 2015 8:05 PM

Gov. John Kasich has really failed on the campaign trail. I thought he would have been far more talented. He is just wasting time & money!

Oct 31, 2015 9:31 PM

I am going to save Medicare and Medicaid, Carson wants to abolish, and failing candidate Gov. John Kasichdoesn't have a clue - weak!

Oct 30, 2015 11:30:23 PM

When candidate John Kasich, on the @oreillyfactor, talked about dismantling Medicare and Medicaid, he was referring to Ben Carson.

Oct 30, 2015 11:20 PM

I now see John Kasich from Ohio- who is desperate to run- is using my line "Make America Great Again". Typical pol- no imagination!

May 20, 2015 9:07 AM

Going to Ohio, home of one of the worst presidential candidates in history--Kasich. Can't debate, loves #ObamaCare--dummy!

Nov 23, 2015 5:11 PM

Rand Paul

Truly weird Senator Rand Paul of Kentucky reminds me of a spoiled brat without a properly functioning brain. He was terrible at DEBATE!

Aug 10, 2015 7:41 PM

Karl Rove

Something must be done with dopey @KarlRove - he is pushing Republicans down the same old path of defeat. Don't fall for it, Karl is a loser

Dec 13, 2015 12:28 AM

Karl Rove --lost GOP both Houses of Congress and the White House--gave us Obama.

Aug 18, 2011 1:01 PM

@KarlRove is a failed Jeb Bushy. Never says anything good & never will. Even after I beat Hillary. Shouldn›t be on the air.

Deleted after 14 minutes at 3:24 PM on May 1, 2016

Dummy @KarlRove continues to make and write false statements. He still thinks Romney won--he should get a life!

Dec 10, 2015 12:53 PM

Republicans must stop relying on losers like @KarlRove if they want to start winning presidential elections. Be tough and get smart! #CrookedHillary

Nov 24, 2015 3:02 PM

Crooked Hillary Again

Crooked Hillary's bad judgement forced her to announce that she would go to Charlotte on Saturday to grandstand. Dem pols said no way, dumb!

Sep 23, 2016 9:09 PM

Remember that Bill Clinton was brought in to help Hillary against Obama in 2008. He was terrible, failed badly, and was called a racist!

Dec 28, 2015 11:31 PM

A massive tax increase will be necessary to fund Crooked Hillary Clinton's agenda. What a terrible (and boring) rollout that was yesterday!

Dec 28, 2015 11:31 PM

Crooked Hillary just can't close the dael with Bernie. It will be the same way with ISIS, and China on trade, and Mexico at the border. Bad!

DELETED AFTER 3 HOURS AT 4:15 PM ON MAY 8, 2016

Amazing that Crooked Hillary can do a hit ad on me concerning women when her husband was the WORST abuser of woman in U.S. political history

MAY 17, 2016 4:58 AM

Crooked Hillary Clinton knew everything that her "servant" was doing at the DNC - they just got caught, that's all! They laughed at Bernie.

JUL 25, 2016 6:19 AM

If Hillary thinks she can unleash her husband, with his terrible record of women abuse, while playing the women's card on me, she's wrong!

DEC 28, 2015 7:12 AM

#CrookedHillary = Obama's third term, which would be terrible news for our economic growth - seen below. https://t.co/y9WJoUaaql

JUL 30, 2016 4:55 PM

So terrible that Crooked didn't report she got the debate questions from Donna Brazile, if that were me it would have been front page news!

NOV 1, 2016 9:14 AM

.@secupp, who can't believe that her candidate has bombed so badly, is one of the dumber pundits on T.V. Hard to watch, zero talent! @CNN

DEC 9, 2015 9:15 PM

Clinton made a false ad about me where I was imitating a reporter GROVELING after he changed his story. I would NEVER Moch disabled. Shame!

DELETED AFTER 22 MINUTES AT 4:20 PM ON JUN 12, 2016

Wow, Crooked Hillary was duped and used by my worst Miss U. Hillary floated her as an "angel" without checking her past, which is terrible!

SEP 30, 2016 4:14 AM

Hillary Clinton just had her 47% moment. What a terrible thing she said about so many great Americans!

SEP 10, 2016 6:37 PM

I employee many people in the State of Virginia - JOBS, JOBS, JOBS! Crooked Hillary will sell us out, just like her husband did with NAFTA.

DELETED AFTER 2 MINUTES AT 1:45 PM ON JUL 14, 2016

Russia has more warheads than ever, N Korea is testing nukes, and Iran got a sweetheart deal to keep theirs. Thanks, @HillaryClinton.

SEP 26, 2016 9:28 PM

Crooked Hillary's V.P. pick said this morning that I was not aware that Russia took over Crimea. A total lie - and taken over during O term

SEP 4, 2016 11:04 AM

Report raises questions about 'Clinton Cash' from Russians during 'reset'

AUG 2, 2016 2:38 PM

Ben Carson

Will miss Ben Carson tonight- at the #GOPDebate. I hope all of Ben's followers will join the #TrumpTrain. M@

DELETED AFTER 55 SECONDS AT 11:04 AM ON MAR 3, 2016

I am seriously considering Dr. Ben Carson as the head of HUD. I've gotten to know him well--he's a greatly talented person who loves people!

NOV 22, 2016 12:10 PM

Dr. Ben Carson- I concur. "I believe in God who can change people-he can make any of us better." @RealBenCarson

MAR 11, 2016 11:44 AM

Ted Cruz has now apologized to Marco Rubio and Ben Carson for fraud and dirty tricks. No wonder he has lost Evangelical support!

FEB 22, 2016 3:55 PM

Dr. Ben Carson blasted Ted Cruz for "deceit and dirty tricks and lies."

FEB 3, 2016 3:44 PM

"@iliveamongyou: @BostonGlobe: Ben Carson advisers say he struggles with foreign policy https://t.co/phTAgT5qP6 https://t.co/044xgNYLth"

NOV 23, 2015 5:26 PM

How does Ben Carson survive this problem – really big. Similar story on front page of New York Times. https://t.co/y9fqUUYRnD

NOV 18, 2015 10:34 AM

.@CarlyFiorina had to inject herself into my factual statements concerning Ben Carson in order to breathe life into her failing campaign!

NOV 13, 2015 3:55 PM

.@CarlyFiorina Ben Carson said in his own book that he has a pathological temper & pathological disease. I didn't say it, he did. Apology?

NOV 13, 2015 03:17 PM

Wow, pres. candidate Ben Carson, who is very weak on illegal Immigration, just said he likes amnesty and a pathway to citizenship.

NOV 12, 2015 2:21 PM

"@Robostop10: @realDonaldTrump This is not good. https://t.co/
lvv0MRfgtH" WOW, one of many lies by Ben Carson! Big story.

Nov 6, 2015 11:46 AM

With Ben Carson wanting to hit his mother on head with a hammer,
stab a friend and Pyramids built for grain storage - don't people get it?

Nov 6, 2015 9:08 AM

Such bad reporting: A puff piece on Ben Carson in the @nytimes
states that Carson "is trying to solidify his lead." But I am #1, easily!
Sad

Nov 6, 2015 7:16 AM

"@DeeMcNa: @FoxNews Silent majority did not try to kill their
mothers, like Ben Carson, but wants America rebuilt by only one
capable:TRUMP"

Nov 6, 2015 4:33 AM

When candidate John Kasich, on the @oreillyfactor, talked about
dismantling Medicare and Medicaid, he was referring to Ben Carson.

Oct 30, 2015 11:20 PM

Ben Carson wants to abolish Medicare - I want to save it and Social
Security.

Oct 25, 2015 7:20 PM

Ben Carson has never created a job in his life (well, maybe a nurse).
I have created tens of thousands of jobs, it's what I do.

Oct 25, 2015 6:41 AM

I spell out some of the differences between Ben Carson and myself
at 9:00 A.M. on @CNN @jaketapper. Ben is very weak on illegal
immigration.

Oct 25, 2015 6:34 AM

Ben Carson was speaking in general terms as to what he would do if confronted with a gunman, and was not criticizing the victims. Not fair!

OCT 7, 2015 6:51 AM

Wow, I am ahead of the field with Evangelicals (am so proud of this) and virtually every other group, and Ben Carson just took a swipe at me

SEP 9, 2015 7:42 PM

.@brithume, I am in first place by a lot in all polls, tied for first place with Ben Carson in one Iowa poll. I thought you knew this-thanks

SEP 2, 2015 9:04 PM

"@JWCarrr: @AnnCoulter @SenTenCes Ben Carson has not criticized Trump! And there's no need to mention Dr. Carson's education!"

JUL 20, 2015 8:51 PM

"@Presidency2016: Dr Ben Carson @RealBenCarson will just need to sweat it out until Donald Trump leaves the White House on 20 January 2025."

MAY 10, 2015 9:32 AM

"@TruthGunner: "@realDonaldTrump: "@dejr5:@realDonaldTrump Donald Trump & Ben Carson 2016" Wow!" I LIKE IT !!! Run Donald, RUN !"

AUG 11, 2014 3:57 AM

«@dejr5: @realDonaldTrump Donald Trump & Ben Carson 2016» Wow!

AUG 9, 2014 2:14 AM

With Dr. Dror Paley & Dr. Ben Carson with two wonderful children at Mar-a-Lago. http://t.co/iw9h3Qa6Y5

APR 2, 2013 11:04 AM

Everybody Calls Him

I have recieved and taken calls from many foreign leaders despite what the failing @nytimes said. Russia, U.K., China, Saudi Arabia, Japan,

Nov 16, 2016 7:17 AM

Yes, it is true - Carlos Slim, the great businessman from Mexico, called me about getting together for a meeting. We met, HE IS A GREAT GUY!

Dec 20, 2016 3:27 PM

Just got a call from my friend Bill Ford, Chairman of Ford, who advised me that he will be keeping the Lincoln plant in Kentucky - no Mexico

Nov 17, 2016 9:01 PM

#MAGA

Why didn't the writer of the twelve year old article in People Magazine mention the "incident" in her story. Because it did not happen

Oct 13, 2016 8:09 AM

.@HillaryClinton #ICYMI- "WE ARE NOT IN A NARRATIVE FIGHT." @Mike_Pence #MAGAhttps://t.co/FUQzXlyPwY

Oct 9, 2016 8:45 PM

The media and establishment want me out of the race so badly - I WILL NEVER DROP OUT OF THE RACE, WILL NEVER LET MY SUPPORTERS DOWN! #MAGA

Oct 8, 2016 2:40 PM

We will bring America together as ONE country again – united as Americans in common purpose and common dreams. #MAGA

Aug 20, 2016 6:11 PM

.@realDonaldTrump stops by overflow room in Mechanicsburg, Pennsylvania- prior to main rally. #TrumpMovement #MAGA

Aug 1, 2016 6:13 PM

"@LinHen23: @foxandfriends Loved Trump's answers to voters questions this morning! Trump's economic plan will help #MAGA #NeverHillary"

AUG 9, 2016 7:02 AM

"@CatOnGlass: 200,000 new followers for @realDonaldTrump. From 10,800,000 to 11,000,000, All in the last ten days or so! #MAGA #AlwaysTrump

AUG 20, 2016 12:02 AM

Second Debate

Hillary Clinton is the only candidate on stage who voted for the Iraq War. #Debates2016 #MAGAhttps://t.co/Um5WJXEEKr

SEP 26, 2016 9:21 PM

I will stand with police and protect ALL Americans! #Debates2016

SEP 26, 2016 8:51 PM

RT @TeamTrump: When @realDonaldTrump is POTUS, families are going to be safe and secure. Law and order will be RESTORED! #MAGA #Debates #De...

SEP 26, 2016 8:50 PM

TIME #DebateNight poll - over 800,000 votes. Thank you! #AmericaFirst #MAGA https://t.co/bTPX9E0wKu

SEP 27, 2016 12:36 AM

Campaign Tweets

In the last 24 hrs. we have raised over $13M from online donations and National Call Day, and we're still going! Thank you America! #MAGA

SEP 27, 2016 2:37 PM

.@realDonaldTrump is going to cut taxes BIG LEAGUE -- Crooked is going to raise taxes BIG LEAGUE! #DrainTheSwamp... https://t.co/41X9Qjy0RJ

OCT 19, 2016 9:32 PM

.@HillaryClinton's tax hikes will CRUSH our economy. I will cut taxes -- BIG LEAGUE. https://t.co/EtA1tBnrNG https://t.co/NgMDP4wiII

OCT 19, 2016 8:42 PM

RT @TeamTrump: RT if you agree @realDonaldTrump WON the #Debate- BIG LEAGUE! #MAGA https://t.co/EmwDZ32uAZ

OCT 9, 2016 9:55 PM

RT @TeamTrump: .@HillaryClinton is RAISING your taxes to a disastrous level. @realDonaldTrump is going to LOWER your taxes - BIG LEAGUE! #D...

OCT 9, 2016 9:02 PM

We're going to cut taxes BIG LEAGUE for the middle class. She's raising your taxes and I'm lowering your taxes! https://t.co/ZwIkqNH2FX

OCT 9, 2016 8:57 PM

.@DRUDGE_REPORT's First Presidential Debate Poll: Trump: 80% Clinton: 20% Join the MOVEMENT today & lets #MAGA!... https://t.co/B12lgC97tn

SEP 27, 2016 12:54 AM

Join me in Colorado Springs, Colorado tomorrow at 1:00pm! #MAGA Tickets: https://t.co/ktFk8RuaUK

OCT 17, 2016 4:38 PM

Departing Farmers Round Table in Boynton Beach, Florida. Get out & VOTE- lets #MAGA! EARLY VOTING BY FL. COUNTY:... https://t.co/MgJxNbxRga

OCT 24, 2016 10:55 AM

In order to #DrainTheSwamp & create a new GOVERNMENT of, by, & for the PEOPLE, I need your VOTE! Go to https://t.co/HfihPERFgZ- LET'S #MAGA!

Oct 22, 2016 2:54 PM

Change has to come from outside our very broken system. #MAGA https://t.co/OH9Lvo3R7K

Oct 22, 2016 1:18 PM

Governor @Mike_Pence and I will be in Cleveland, Ohio tomorrow night at 7pm - join us! #MAGA Tickets:... https://t.co/kfJv5Po0x6

Oct 21, 2016 9:41 PM

Thank you to the great crowd of supporters in Newtown, Pennsylvania. Get out & VOTE on 11/8/16. Lets #MAGA! Watch:... https://t.co/eb6XuMlbFW

Oct 21, 2016 7:58 PM

Thank you America! #MAGA Rasmussen National Poll Donald Trump 43% Hillary Clinton 40% https://t.co/n4eZ3qpcjg

Oct 20, 2016 8:27 AM

Join the MOVEMENT to #MAGA! https://t.co/3KWOl2ibaW https://t.co/V84qfN4oz1

Oct 19, 2016 11:10 PM

Great poll - thank you America! Once we #DrainTheSwamp, together we will #MAGA⊠#Debate https://t.co/SvcjmrsHKD

Oct 19, 2016 11:06 PM

I started this campaign to Make America Great Again. That's what I'm going to do. #MAGA #debate

Oct 19, 2016 9:39 PM

Loved the debate last night, and almost everyone said I won, but the RNC did a terrible job of ticket distrbution. All donors & special ints

Feb 14, 2016 3:55 PM

Bernie Sanders

There is no longer a Bernie Sanders "political revolution." He is turning out to be a weak and somewhat pathetic figure,wants it all to end!

Jul 24, 2016 9:27 AM

The race for DNC Chairman was, of course, totally "rigged." Bernie's guy, like Bernie himself, never had a chance. Clinton demanded Perez!

Feb 26, 2017 6:33 AM

While on FAKE NEWS @CNN, Bernie Sanders was cut off for using the term fake news to describe the network. They said technical difficulties!

Feb 12, 2017 7:14 AM

"@jensen4law: Best way to pay Hillary back for what she did to @BernieSanders #DNCleak is a DonaldTrump LANDSLIDE https://t.co/Ha8o5wCyGh"

Oct 22, 2016 6:35 AM

Bernie Sanders on HRC: Bad Judgement. John Podesta on HRC: Bad Instincts. #BigLeagueTruth #Debate

Oct 19, 2016 9:19 PM

Wow, @CNN Town Hall questions were given to Crooked Hillary Clinton in advance of big debates against Bernie Sanders. Hillary & CNN FRAUD!

Oct 11, 2016 6:04 PM

With the exception of cheating Bernie out of the nom the Dems have always proven to be far more loyal to each other than the Republicans!

Oct 11, 2016 9:15 AM

Bernie should pull his endorsement of Crooked Hillary after she decieved him and then attacked him and his supporters.

OCT 2, 2016 4:48 PM

Bernie Sanders gave Hillary the Dem nomination when he gave up on the e-mails. That issue has only gotten bigger!

SEP 25, 2016 8:04 AM

Many on the team and staff of Bernie Sanders have been treated badly by the Hillary Clinton campaign - and they like Trump on trade, a lot!

SEP 25, 2016 7:30 AM

Crooked Hillary's brainpower is highly overrated.Probably why her decision making is so bad or, as stated by Bernie S, she has BAD JUDGEMENT

AUG 29, 2016 8:30 AM

"@GoldJazz559: #BlackMenForBernie Leader: #Hillary2016 'No Regard For Black Race' https://t.co/m8952Ly3Jb via @dailycaller #BlacksForTrump

AUG 27, 2016 10:18 AM

President Obama should ask the DNC about how they rigged the election against Bernie.

AUG 4, 2016 9:18 PM

Hillary can never win over Bernie supporters. Her foreign wars, NAFTA/TPP support & Wall Street ties are driving away millions of votes.

JUL 30, 2016 7:54 AM

As usual, Hillary & the Dems are trying to rig the debates so 2 are up against major NFL games. Same as last time w/ Bernie. Unacceptable!

JUL 29, 2016 10:03 PM

What Bernie Sanders really thinks of Crooked Hillary Clinton. https://t.co/VgMaAsZBep

> Jul 29, 2016 12:53 PM

Wow, my campaign is hearing from more and more Bernie supporters that they will NEVER support Crooked Hillary. She sold them out, V.P. pick!

> Jul 29, 2016 12:03 PM

The dishonest media didn't mention that Bernie Sanders was very angry looking during Crooked's speech. He wishes he didn't make that deal!

> Jul 29, 2016 11:56 AM

Bernie caved! https://t.co/xtcOnA8cw1

> Jul 28, 2016 1:36 PM

Many of Bernie's supporters have left the arena. Did Bernie go home and go to sleep?

> Jul 26, 2016 9:11 PM

Bernie's exhausted, he just wants to shut down and go home to bed!

> Jul 26, 2016 2:27 PM

Bernie Sanders totally sold out to Crooked Hillary Clinton. All of that work, energy and money, and nothing to show for it! Waste of time.

> Jul 25, 2016 10:19 PM

Sad to watch Bernie Sanders abandon his revolution. We welcome all voters who want to fix our rigged system and bring back our jobs.

> Jul 25, 2016 10:04 PM

Hard to believe that Bernie Sanders has done such a complete fold. He got NOTHING for all of the time, energy and money. The V.P. a joke!

> Jul 25, 2016 4:45 PM

While Bernie has totally given up on his fight for the people, we welcome all voters who want a better future for our workers.

JUL 25, 2016 4:33 PM

Clinton betrayed Bernie voters. Kaine supports TPP, is in pocket of Wall Street, and backed Iraq War.

JUL 25, 2016 4:32 PM

Crooked Hillary Clinton knew everything that her "servant" was doing at the DNC - they just got caught, that's all! They laughed at Bernie.

JUL 25, 2016 8:19 AM

If Bernie Sanders, after seeing the just released e-mails, continues to look exhausted and done, then his legacy will never be the same.

JUL 25, 2016 7:27 AM

How much BAD JUDGEMENT was on display by the people in DNC in writing those really dumb e-mails, using even religion, against Bernie!

JUL 25, 2016 6:57 AM

Even though Bernie Sanders has lost his energy and his strength, I don't believe that his supporters will let Crooked Hillary off the hook!

JUL 24, 2016 5:07 PM

Crooked Hillary Clinton was not at all loyal to the person in her rigged system that pushed her over the top, DWS. Too bad Bernie flamed out

JUL 24, 2016 5:02 PM

If the Republican Convention had blown up with e-mails, resignation of boss and the beat down of a big player. (Bernie), media would go wild

JUL 24, 2016 4:53 PM

I always said that Debbie Wasserman Schultz was overrated. The Dems Convention is cracking up and Bernieis exhausted, no energy left!

JUL 24, 2016 3:30 PM

Sorry folks, but Bernie Sanders is exhausted, just can't go on any longer. He is trying to dismiss the new e-mails and DNC disrespect. SAD!

JUL 24, 2016 8:30 AM

There is no longer a Bernie Sanders "political revolution." He is turning out to be a weak and somewhat pathetic figure,wants it all to end!

JUL 24, 2016 8:27 AM

An analysis showed that Bernie Sanders would have won the Democratic nomination if it were not for the Super Delegates.

JUL 24, 2016 7:30 AM

Looks like the Bernie people will fight. If not, their BLOOD, SWEAT AND TEARS was a total waste of time. Kaine stands for opposite!

JUL 24, 2016 7:15 AM

Bernie Sanders started off strong, but with the selection of Kaine for V.P., is ending really weak. So much for a movement! TOTAL DISRESPECT

JUL 24, 2016 6:25 AM

The Crooked Hillary V.P. choice is VERY disrespectful to Bernie Sanders and all of his supporters. Just another case of BAD JUDGEMENT by H!

JUL 24, 2016 6:16 AM

Leaked e-mails of DNC show plans to destroy Bernie Sanders. Mock his heritage and much more. On-line from Wikileakes, really vicious. RIGGED

JUL 23, 2016 5:55 AM

Tim Kaine is, and always has been, owned by the banks. Bernie supporters are outraged, was their last choice. Bernie fought for nothing!

JUL 23, 2016 5:35 AM

The Bernie Sanders supporters are furious with the choice of Tim Kaine, who represents the opposite of what Bernie stands for. Philly fight?

JUL 23, 2016 5:31 AM

It doesn't matter that Crooked Hillary has experience, look at all of the bad decisions she has made. Berniesaid she has bad judgement!

JUL 17, 2016 7:06 AM

To all the Bernie voters who want to stop bad trade deals & global special interests, we welcome you with open arms. People first.

JUL 12, 2016 12:04 PM

Bernie sanders has abandoned his supporters by endorsing pro-war pro-TPP pro-Wall Street Crooked Hillary Clinton.

JUL 12, 2016 12:03 PM

Bernie Sanders endorsing Crooked Hillary Clinton is like Occupy Wall Street endorsing Goldman Sachs.

JUL 12, 2016 12:01 PM

I am somewhat surprised that Bernie Sanders was not true to himself and his supporters. They are not happy that he is selling out!

JUL 12, 2016 8:39 AM

Bernie Sanders, who has lost most of his leverage, has totally sold out to Crooked Hillary Clinton. He will endorse her today - fans angry!

JUL 12, 2016 8:36 AM

As Bernie Sanders said, Hillary Clinton has bad judgement. Bill's meeting was probably initiated and demanded by Hillary!

JUL 1, 2016 7:11 AM

Bernie Sanders must really dislike Crooked Hillary after the way she played him. Many of his supporters, because of trade, will come to me.

JUN 8, 2016 8:46 PM

Bernie Sanders was right when he said that Crooked Hillary Clinton was not qualified to be president because she suffers from BAD judgement!

JUN 2, 2016 10:10 AM

Crooked Hillary Clinton just can't close the deal with Bernie. I had to knock out 16 very good and smart candidates. Hillary doesn't have it

MAY 25, 2016 8:14 AM

Bernie Sanders is continuing his quest because he believes that Crooked Hillary Clinton will be forced out of the race - e-mail scandal!

MAY 22, 2016 3:32 PM

Crooked Hillary can't even close the deal with Bernie - and the Dems have it rigged in favor of Hillary. Four more years of this? No way!

MAY 20, 2016 5:26 AM

I said that Crooked Hillary Clinton is "not qualified" to be president because she has "very bad judgement" - Bernie said the same thing!

MAY 20, 2016 4:40 AM

Bernie Sanders is being treated very badly by the Democrats - the system is rigged against him. Many of his disenfranchised fans are for me!

MAY 18, 2016 6:20 AM

"@ShoneeP: @realDonaldTrump Trump for President! Bernie is a joke, knows nothing - and Hillary is yesterday's and today's nightmare"

MAY 17, 2016 11:03 PM

"@HFFoundation4: @realDonaldTrump One thing we know for sure @BernieSanders supporters will turn to #Trump - absolutely not @HillaryClinton"

MAY 17, 2016 7:28 PM

Crooked Hillary can't close the deal with Bernie Sanders. Will be another bad day for her!

MAY 17, 2016 7:31 AM

Bernie Sanders is being treated very badly by the Dems. The system is rigged against him. He should run as an independent! Run Bernie, run.

MAY 16, 2016 5:00 AM

If Crooked Hillary Clinton can't close the deal on Crazy Bernie, how is she going to take on China, Russia, ISIS and all of the others?

MAY 13, 2016 8:03 PM

I don't want to hit Crazy Bernie Sanders too hard yet because I love watching what he is doing to Crooked Hillary. His time will come!

MAY 11, 2016 5:26 AM

Big wins in West Virginia and Nebraska. Get ready for November - Crooked Hillary, who is looking very bad against Crazy Bernie, will lose!

MAY 11, 2016 5:22 AM

Crooked Hillary just can't close the deal with Bernie. It will be the same way with ISIS, and China on trade, and Mexico at the border. Bad!

MAY 8, 2016 3:15 PM

Crooked Hillary has ZERO leadership ability. As Bernie Sanders says, she has bad judgement. Constantly playing the women's card - it is sad!

MAY 6, 2016 7:38 AM

Bernie Sanders has been treated terribly by the Democrats—both with delegates & otherwise. He should show them, & run as an Independent.

MAY 5, 2016 2:30 PM

I would rather run against Crooked Hillary Clinton than Bernie Sanders and that will happen because the books are cooked against Bernie!

MAY 4, 2016 4:44 AM

Bernie Sanders has been treated terribly by the Democrats—both with delegates & otherwise. He should show them, and run as an Independent!

APR 26, 2016 11:07 AM

I would have millions of votes more than Hillary except for the fact that I had 17 opponents and she just had a socialist named Bernie!

APR 17, 2016 9:34 AM

Bernie Sanders says that Hillary Clinton is unqualified to be president. Based on her decision making ability, I can go along with that!

APR 9, 2016 6:22 AM

How come the @TODAYshow & @chucktodd show the new @NBCNews Poll for Hillary vs Bernie but do not show the SAME poll where I am killing Cruz?

MAR 29, 2016 9:45 AM

«@wh: https://t.co/AZmCErLKCn WOW people are so misinformed on DonaldTrump character! Watch this video! Hillary and Bernie don›t come close

MAR 14, 2016 10:44 PM

Bernie Sanders is lying when he says his disruptors aren't told to go to my events. Be careful Bernie, or my supporters will go to yours!

MAR 13, 2016 6:48 AM

The last person that Hillary or Bernie want to run against is Donald Trump --- and that is fact!

MAR 12, 2016 1:24 PM

.@USATODAY Poll and @QuinnipiacPoll say that I beat both Hillary and Bernie, and I havn't even started on them yet!

FEB 24, 2016 11:12 AM

The just out USA Today National Poll, where I lead by big numbers, shows that in a head to head matchup, I beat both Hillary and Bernie.

FEB 18, 2016 5:53 AM

"@MarkHalperin: My report card grades for the 2 New Hampshire winners: DonaldTrump A: v strong energy/close. BernieSanders B+: went too long

FEB 10, 2016 12:11 AM

"@MrJuuon: #WeAreBernie will be overtaken by #WeWantTrump. We are superior and have more supporters. #makeamericagreatagain #trump."

JAN 24, 2016 11:05 PM

"@deggow: Just heard a 25 year old man say "I would rather work for Donald Trump than Bernie Sanders"it's time for me to leave this party."

DEC 31, 2015 5:53 AM

Strange, but I see wacko Bernie Sanders allies coming over to me because I'm lowering taxes, while he will double & triple them, a disaster!

DEC 28, 2015 8:34 AM

.@BernieSanders-who blew his campaign when he gave Hillary a pass on her e-mail crime, said that I feel wages in America are too high. Lie!

DEC 27, 2015 11:49 AM

"@BernieSanders: ABC News spent 81 minutes on Donald Trump and only 20 seconds on our campaign. That's because @ABC is smart!

DEC 13, 2015 12:31 PM

Wow, Bernie Sanders just admitted that the real unemployment rate is 10% (it is actually over 20%) and for African American youth - 51%.

NOV 14, 2015 10:52 PM

"@muhfuck: @BernieSanders Donald Trump is the only candidate for middle class America @realDonaldTrump #Trump2016 #MakeAmericaGreatAgain"

OCT 18, 2015 4:10 PM

Good move by Bernie S.

OCT 13, 2015 8:55 PM

How is Bernie Sanders going to defend our country if he can't even defend his own microphone? Very sad!

AUG 22, 2015 3:23 PM

Bernie Voters

Looks to me like the Bernie people will fight. If not, there blood, sweat and tears was a total waist of time. Kaine stands for opposite!

DELETED AFTER 39 MINUTES AT 8:26 PM ON JUL 24, 2016

The Wikileakes e-mail release today was so bad to Sanders that it will make it impossible for him to support her, unless he is a fraud!

DELETED AFTER 18 MINUTES AT 11:25 AM ON JUL 24, 2016

How much BAD JUDGEMENT was on display by the people in DNC in writing those really dumb e-mails, using even religion, against Bernie!

JUL 25, 2016 6:57 AM

No complaints but how many people would be watching these really dumb but record setting debates if I wasn't in them? Interesting question!

OCT 31, 2015 5:31 PM

The money losing @politico is considered by many in the world of politics to be the dumbest and most slanted of the political sites. Losers!

OCT 29, 2015 5:47 AM

Dopey @BillKristol, who has lost all credibility with so many dumb statements and picks, said last week on @Morning_Joe that Biden was in.

OCT 26, 2015 5:19 PM

Make America Safe Again

Saturday's attacks show that failed Obama/Hillary Clinton polices won't keep us safe! I will Make America Safe Again!

DELETED AFTER 10 HOURS AT 9:18 AM ON SEP 19, 2016

News Coverage

.@CNN just doesn't get it, and that's why their ratings are so low - and getting worse. Boring anti-Trump panelists, mostly losers in life!

SEP 17, 2016 8:13 AM

Thank you for your incredible support Wisconsin and Governor @ScottWalker! It is time to #DrainTheSwamp & #MAGA!... https://t.co/gKBkKmTudn

NOV 1, 2016 7:32 PM

Join @TeamTrump on Facebook & watch tonight's rally from Geneva, Ohio- our 3rd rally of the day. #AmericaFirst #MAGA https://t.co/ZqJmf4QcwH

OCT 27, 2016 7:14 PM

I delivered a speech in Charlotte, North Carolina yesterday. I appreciate all of the feedback & support. Lets #MAGA… https://t.co/aI2HtiRUzr

OCT 27, 2016 5:05 PM

Join me live in Toledo, Ohio. Time to #DrainTheSwamp & #MAGA! https://t.co/NU39Mmlh1T

OCT 27, 2016 4:07 PM

Join me in Cedar Rapids, Iowa tomorrow at 7:00pm! #MAGA https://t.co/QWaEJpzvKN https://t.co/CniHGkjp0v

OCT 27, 2016 4:02 PM

JOIN ME! #MAGA TODAY: Springfield, OH Toledo, OH Geneva, OH FRIDAY: Manchester, NH Lisbon, ME Cedar Rapids, IA https://t.co/kv624y9UOm

OCT 27, 2016 9:44 AM

CHAPTER 14

Endorsements

"@Michael_0000: [First Vote News Video | Mike Tyson Endorses Donald Trump for President] - https://t.co/7c0VeVj5ko" Thanks Mike!

Nov 1, 2015 7:17 AM

"@julian771177: Mike Tyson endorses @realDonaldTrump https://t.co/rKMkXAFeop #MakeAmericaGreatAgain" Thanks Iron Mike, greatly appreciated!

Oct 26, 2015 10:32 PM

Just finished the wonderful event on the U.S.S. Iowa. VETERANS FOR A STRONG AMERICA endorsed me. Such a great honor, thank you!

Sep 15, 2015 9:39 PM

"@suzost: UFC President Dana White Endorses Donald Trump [VIDEO] https://t.co/MwQtFzuDpY via @dailycaller" Love this from a real winner!

Dec 13, 2015 9:57 PM

"@TheProdigy3D: Everyone vote for @realDonaldTrump and no he did not pay me for this endorsement."

DEC 13, 2015 5:18 PM

Great evening last night in New Hampshire. Got the endorsement from the New England Police Union - big territory, great people! Thank you.

DEC 11, 2015 6:34 AM

An honor to be endorsed by the New England Police Benevolent Association. Thank you! https://t.co/zj47db1Yj1 https://t.co/JrjHyLRkD6

DEC 10, 2015 8:10 PM

"@DanScavino: Bruce LeVell, former GOP Chairman of Gwinnett County (GA) endorsed @realDonaldTrump today. #TeamTrump https://t.co/OY4Uo3tcJu

DEC 2, 2015 6:42 PM

"@ghosthunter_lol: Iowa key endorsement for @realDonaldTrump Can't wait for the Iowa caucus in 4 weeks! #Trump2016 https://t.co/JBfyFrZfFb"

JAN 4, 2016 10:42 PM

I hope all workers demand that their @Teamsters reps endorse Donald J. Trump. Nobody knows jobs like I do! Don't let them sell you out!

JAN 8, 2016 5:03 PM

If their highly unethical behavior, including begging me for ads, isn't questionable enough, they have endorsed a candidate who can't win.

JAN 10, 2016 4:06 PM

A true honor to receive the endorsement of John Wayne's daughter....read: https://t.co/X6jR0WVBvd https://t.co/1e6gk0PsQH

JAN 19, 2016 1:11 PM

I am greatly honored to receive Sarah Palin's endorsement tonight. Video: https://t.co/4P7AMKI4iq https://t.co/bjTPvwM4nW

JAN 19, 2016 11:05 PM

"@nytimes: Breaking News: Sarah Palin has endorsed Donald Trump in the GOP primary - appeal to Tea Party loyalists https://t.co/9aKuuuD1wE"

JAN 20, 2016 6:16 AM

"National Black Republican Association Endorses Donald J. Trump" #Trump2016 #MakeAmericaGreatAgain https://t.co/9IPw30G5OG

JAN 22, 2016 4:39 PM

.@williebosshog such an honor to get your endorsement. You are a fantastic guy! It will not be forgotten. Don and Eric say hello!

JAN 23, 2016 3:28 PM

Great honor- Rev. Jerry Falwell Jr. of Liberty University, one of the most respected religious leaders in our nation, has just endorsed me!

JAN 26, 2016 11:55 AM

So nice to get an endorsement from the founder and owner of Pizza Ranch in Iowa! A great guy and great places! #CaucusForTrump

JAN 31, 2016 11:47 AM

Thank you for your endorsement @paulteutulsr! #BikersForTrump #VoteTrumpNV Video: https://t.co/1JEdwPPCux https://t.co/56gkQTM7oc

FEB 22, 2016 1:54 PM

.@RepChrisCollins Chris, thank you so much for your wonderful endorsement. I will not let you down! @CNN

FEB 24, 2016 8:08 PM

When Mitt Romney asked me for my endorsement last time around, he was so awkward and goofy that we all should have known he could not win!

Feb 24, 2016 6:26 PM

Why doesn't @MittRomney just endorse @marcorubio already. Should have done it before NH or Nevada where he had a little sway. Too late now!

Feb 25, 2016 11:05 AM

Great news- Former Mayor of Dallas, Tom Leppert, has just endorsed me! Thank you! Tomorrow is a big day- VOTE! #VoteTrump #SuperTuesday

Feb 29, 2016 8:40 PM

Got the endorsement of Brian France and @NASCAR yesterday in Georgia. Also, many of the sports great drivers. Thank you Nascar and Georgia!

Mar 1, 2016 6:15 AM

It means so much to me- receiving an endorsement from Phyllis Schlafly. A truly great woman & conservative. https://t.co/11rEMu99qc

Mar 11, 2016 5:40 PM

Thank you to the Governor of Florida, Rick Scott, for your endorsement. I greatly appreciate your support!

Mar 16, 2016 12:14 PM

"@DonaldJTrumpJr: Honored to be in #Utah with retired General Robert C. Oaks. We are so thankful for his support and endorsement here in SLC

Mar 19, 2016 7:15 AM

"@Veteran4Trump: Vets For A Strong America Endorses Donald Trump for president; "We've Endorsed Him, We Believe In Him" #Trump2016

MAR 19, 2016 2:09 AM

"@WesleyRickard: Sheriff Joe Arpaio AZ Endorses Donald J Trump for President of the United States #AZ #UT https://t.co/4FzcTZIGqE"

MAR 19, 2016 2:00 AM

For the 1st time in American history, America's 16,500 border patrol agents have issue a presidential primary endorsement—me! Thank you.

APR 1, 2016 9:25 AM

"@kirstiealley: HELLO BOYS! this is my formal endorsement of @realDonaldTrump & I'm a woman! (last I checked) And Rudy, U R amazing!

APR 8, 2016 8:54 PM

Thank you for today's endorsement, New York Veteran Police Association! #NewYorkValues https://t.co/AMFBymUXuZ https://t.co/ZQHmkBDUnA

APR 17, 2016 6:04 PM

Getting the strong endorsement of the great coach, Bobby Knight, has been a highlight of my stay in Indiana. Big speech tomorrow with Bobby!

APR 27, 2016 10:49 PM

Thank you for the endorsement, Coach Bobby Knight! I will never forget it! https://t.co/FchYdKY4F8 https://t.co/MpRtRwv51u

APR 27, 2016 8:47 PM

I will be in Evansville, Indiana, with the great Bobby Knight (who last night endorsed me) at 12:00 this afternoon. See you there!

Apr 28, 2016 7:14 AM

Honored to have received the endorsement of Lou Holtz - a great guy! #INPrimary #Trump2016 https://t.co/AeGyODb37O

May 2, 2016 2:57 PM

Joe Scarborough initially endorsed Jeb Bush and Jeb crashed, then John Kasich and that didn't work. Not much power or insight!

May 6, 2016 1:03 PM

So many great endorsements yesterday, except for Paul Ryan! We must put America first and MAKE AMERICA GREAT AGAIN!

May 6, 2016 5:26 AM

An incredible honor to receive the endorsement of a person I have such tremendous respect for. Thank you, Sheldon! https://t.co/nW0N3OO4mw

May 13, 2016 3:31 PM

Thank you for your wonderful endorsement today @TGowdySC. It means a great deal to me. We will not disappoint! #Trump2016

May 20, 2016 5:50 PM

Thank you! An honor to be the first candidate ever endorsed by the @NRA- prior to @GOPconvention! #Trump2016 #2A https://t.co/ygLUAl7gzx

May 20, 2016 3:06 PM

Thank you! An honor to be the first candidate ever endorsed by the @NRA- prior to @GOPconvention! #Trump2016 #2A https://t.co/ygLUAl7gzx

May 20, 2016 3:06 PM

Great honor to receive today's endorsement of @RickSantorum. Really nice! #Trump2016

MAY 24, 2016 7:33 PM

In getting the endorsement of the 16,500 Border Patrol Agents (thank you), the statement was made that the WALL was very necessary!

MAY 30, 2016 6:00 AM

The endorsement of me by the 16,500 Border Patrol Agents was the first time that they ever endorsed a presidential candidate. Nice!

MAY 30, 2016 6:05 AM

So great to have the endorsement and support of Paul Ryan. We will both be working very hard to Make America Great Again!

JUN 2, 2016 4:12 PM

Obama just endorsed Crooked Hillary. He wants four more years of Obama—but nobody else does!

JUN 9, 2016 1:22 PM

Truly honored to receive the first ever presidential endorsement from the Bay of Pigs Veterans Association. #MAGA… https://t.co/aRdlFkVjAx

OCT 25, 2016 1:27 PM

Bernie Sanders, who has lost most of his leverage, has totally sold out to Crooked Hillary Clinton. He will endorse her today - fans angry!

JUL 12, 2016 8:36 AM

CHAPTER 15

Since Becoming President

Despite the odds (many of which he himself drew attention to via Twitter), Donald Trump was elected president on November 8, 2016. Many expected him to slow down his constant tweeting once he became president, but that did not happen. Some think he has the right to express his opinion on Twitter even as president—the right to fire back at detractors—and others believe his tweeting is beneath the office of the president. But it doesn't matter what either side says—because he just keeps tweeting on.

@DonaldJTrumpJr: FINAL PUSH! Eric and I doing dozens of radio interviews. We can win this thing! GET OUT AND VOTE! #MAGA #ElectionDay ht...

Nov 8, 2016 6:20 PM

RT @DonaldJTrumpJr: Thanks New Hampshire!!! #NH #New-Hampshire #MAGA https://t.co/JDgcyJvJpk

Nov 7, 2016 11:29 PM

LIVE on #Periscope: Join me for a few minutes in Pennsylvania. Get out & VOTE tomorrow. LETS #MAGA!! https://t.co/Ej0LmMK3YU

Nov 7, 2016 6:28 PM

Thank you Pennsylvania- I am forever grateful for your amazing support. Lets MAKE AMERICA GREAT AGAIN! #MAGA... https://t.co/qbcJZAzw6z

Nov 6, 2016 11:14 PM

Thank you Minnesota! It is time to #DrainTheSwamp & #MAGA! #ICYMI- watch: https://t.co/fVThC7yIL6 https://t.co/e8SaXiJrxj

Nov 6, 2016 6:42 PM

Thank you Hershey, Pennsylvania. Get out & VOTE on November 8th & we will #MAGA! #RallyForRiley #ICYMI, watch here... https://t.co/maWukVBTr8

Nov 4, 2016 9:52 PM

Watching the returns at 9:45pm. #ElectionNight #MAGA⬛⬛ https://t.co/HfuJeRZbod

Nov 8, 2016 9:48 PM

If my many supporters acted and threatened people like those who lost the election are doing, they would be scorned & called terrible names!

Dec 18, 2016 4:54 PM

The "Intelligence" briefing on so-called "Russian hacking" was delayed until Friday, perhaps more time needed to build a case. Very strange!

Jan 3, 2017 8:14 PM

The opinion of this so-called judge, which essentially takes law-enforcement away from our country, is ridiculous and will be overturned!

Feb 4, 2017 8:12 AM

The so-called "A" list celebrities are all wanting tixs to the inauguration, but look what they did for Hillary, NOTHING. I want the PEOPLE!

Dec 22, 2016 8:59 PM

Reports by @CNN that I will be working on The Apprentice during my Presidency, even part time, are rediculous & untrue - FAKE NEWS!

DELETED AFTER 2 HOURS AT 9:11 AM ON DEC 10, 2016

Somebody hacked the DNC but why did they not have "hacking defense" like the RNC has and why have they not responded to the terrible......

JAN 4, 2017 8:27 AM

It would have been much easier for me to win the so-called popular vote than the Electoral College in that I would only campaign in 3 or 4--

NOV 27, 2016 3:34 PM

Victory Tour Announcements

RT @DanScavino: Join #PEOTUS Trump & #VPEOTUS Pence live in West Allis, Wisconsin! #ThankYouTour2016 #MAGA https://t.co/vU5EPIYKUc https:/...

DEC 13, 2016 7:52 PM

Join me tomorrow! #MAGA 10am- Baton Rouge, LA. Tickets: https://t.co/rvIQ6Yq45P 7pm- Grand Rapids, MI. Tickets: https://t.co/2UTwAg5V87

DEC 8, 2016 6:12 PM

Join me tomorrow in Des Moines, Iowa with Vice President-Elect @mike_pence - at 7:00pm! #ThankYouTour2016 #MAGA... https://t.co/Geq6sT70IT

DEC 7, 2016 2:37 PM

My transition team, which is working long hours and doing a fantastic job, will be seeing many great candidates today. #MAGA

NOV 17, 2016 7:46 AM

The world was gloomy before I won - there was no hope. Now the market is up nearly 10% and Christmasspending is over a trillion dollars!

Dec 26, 2016 6:32 PM

"Unpresidented"

China steals United States Navy research drone in international waters - rips it out of water and takes it to China in unpresidented act.

Deleted after 1 hour at 9:06 AM on Dec 17, 2016

Named Person of the Year

Remember, get TIME magazine! I am on the cover. Take it out in 4 years and read it again! Just watch...

Jan 10, 2016 3:15 PM

(1/2) Time Magazine has me on the cover this week. David Von Drehle has written one of the best stories I have ever had.

Jan 9, 2016 12:56 PM

Thank you to Time Magazine and Financial Times for naming me "Person of the Year" - a great honor!

Dec 15, 2016 8:09 AM

Promises

We will follow two simple rules: BUY AMERICAN & HIRE AMERICAN! #InaugurationDay #MAGA🇺🇸

Jan 20, 2017 12:55 PM

Mexico has taken advantage of the U.S. for long enough. Massive trade deficits & little help on the very weak border must change, NOW!

Jan 27, 2017 8:19 AM

of jobs and companies lost. If Mexico is unwilling to pay for the badly needed wall, then it would be better to cancel the upcoming meeting.

Jan 26, 2017 8:55 AM

Dishonest media says Mexico won't be paying for the wall if they pay a little later so the wall can be built more quickly. Media is fake!

JAN 8, 2017 11:05 PM

The dishonest media does not report that any money spent on building the Great Wall (for sake of speed), will be paid back by Mexico later!

JAN 6, 2017 6:19 AM

much worse - just look at Syria (red line), Crimea, Ukraine and the build-up of Russian nukes. Not good! Was this the leaker of Fake News?

JAN 15, 2017 7:29 PM

Mexico was just ranked the second deadliest country in the world, after only Syria. Drug trade is largely the cause. We will BUILD THE WALL!

JUN 22, 2017 3:15 PM

Car Talk

Toyota Motor said will build a new plant in Baja, Mexico, to build Corolla cars for U.S. NO WAY! Build plant in U.S. or pay big border tax.

JAN 5, 2017 1:14 PM

Great meeting with automobile industry leaders at the @WhiteHouse this morning. Together, we will #MAGA! https://t.co/OXdiLOkGsZ

JAN 24, 2017 12:04 PM

(1/2) Totally biased @NBCNews went out of its way to say that the big announcement from Ford, G.M., Lockheed & others that jobs are coming back...

JAN 18, 2017 4:34 AM

(2/2) to the U.S., but had nothing to do with TRUMP, is more FAKE NEWS. Ask top CEO's of those companies for real facts. Came back because of me!

JAN 18, 2017 4:44 AM

Russia

Russia talk is FAKE NEWS put out by the Dems, and played up by the media, in order to mask the big election defeat and the illegal leaks

FEB 26, 2017 1:16 PM

This Russian connection non-sense is merely an attempt to cover-up the many mistakes made in Hillary Clinton's losing campaign.

FEB 15, 2017 7:08 AM

Totally made up facts by sleazebag political operatives, both Democrats and Republicans - FAKE NEWS! Russiasays nothing exists. Probably...

JAN 13, 2017 6:11 AM

Russia has never tried to use leverage over me. I HAVE NOTHING TO DO WITH RUSSIA - NO DEALS, NO LOANS, NO NOTHING!

JAN 11, 2017 7:31 AM

Russia just said the unverified report paid for by political opponents is "A COMPLETE AND TOTAL FABRICATION, UTTER NONSENSE." Very unfair!

JAN 11, 2017 7:13 AM

'BuzzFeed Runs Unverifiable Trump-Russia Claims' #FakeNews

JAN 10, 2017 9:00 PM

Having a good relationship with Russia is a good thing, not a bad thing. Only "stupid" people, or fools, would think that it is bad!

JAN 7, 2017 10:02 AM

The Democratic National Committee would not allow the FBI to study or see its computer info after it was supposedly hacked by Russia......

> JAN 5, 2017 7:30 PM

I don't know Putin, have no deals in Russia, and the haters are going crazy - yet Obama can make a deal with Iran, #1in terror, no problem!

> FEB 7, 2017 7:04 AM

I don't know Putin, have no deals in Russia, and the haters are going crazy - yet Obama can make a deal with Iran, #1 in terror, no problem! (same tweet, different time)

> FEB 7, 2017 7:11 AM *(SAME TWEET, DIFFERENT TIME)*

Julian Assange said "a 14 year old could have hacked Podesta" - why was DNC so careless? Also said Russians did not give him the info!

> JAN 4, 2017 7:22 AM

The Travel/Muslim Ban

Interesting that certain Middle-Eastern countries agree with the ban. They know if certain people are allowed in it's death & destruction!

> FEB 4, 2017 8:06 AM

SEE YOU IN COURT, THE SECURITY OF OUR NATION IS AT STAKE!

> FEB 9, 2017 3:35 PM

The threat from radical Islamic terrorism is very real, just look at what is happening in Europe and the Middle-East. Courts must act fast!

> FEB 6, 2017 6:49 PM

72% of refugees admitted into U.S. (2/3 -2/11) during COURT BREAKDOWN are from 7 countries: SYRIA, IRAQ, SOMALIA, IRAN, SUDAN, LIBYA & YEMEN

FEB 12, 2017 3:55 AM

The crackdown on illegal criminals is merely the keeping of my campaign promise. Gang members, drug dealers & others are being removed!

FEB 12, 2017 3:34 AM

First the Ninth Circuit rules against the ban & now it hits again on sanctuary cities-both ridiculous rulings. See you in the Supreme Court!

APR 26, 2017 5:20 AM

Out of our very big country, with many choices, does everyone notice that both the "ban" case and now the "sanctuary" case is brought in ...

APR 26, 2017 5:30 AM

...the Ninth Circuit, which has a terrible record of being overturned (close to 80%). They used to call this "judge shopping!" Messy system.

APR 26, 2017 5:38 AM

Well, as predicted, the 9th Circuit did it again - Ruled against the TRAVEL BAN at such a dangerous time in the history of our country. S.C.

JUN 13, 2017 3:44 AM

"Paid" Protesters Cabinet Members, and Polls (Oh My)

RT @EricTrump: BREAKING: Anti-Trump Protesters Admit They Were Hired on Craigslist – Being PAID to Protest https://t.co/eJ2MRMXyMo via @rightwingnews

DELETED AFTER 1 MINUTE AT 2:02 AM ON MAR 24, 2017.
ORIGINAL TWEET BY @ERICTRUMP.

It is Clinton and Sanders people who disrupted my rally in Chicago - and then they say I must talk to my people. Phony politicions!

DELETED AFTER 33 MINUTES AT 4:01 PM ON MAR 12, 2017

The Cabinet

Retweet from Eva Moskowitz: .@BetsyDeVos has the talent, commitment, and leadership capacity to revitalize our public schools and deliver the promise of opportunity.

JAN 17, 2017 9:08 AM

The same people who did the phony election polls, and were so wrong, are now doing approval rating polls. They are rigged just like before.

JAN 17, 2017 5:11 AM

People are pouring into Washington in record numbers. Bikers for Trump are on their way. It will be a great Thursday, Friday and Saturday!

JAN 17, 2017 5:05 AM

SNL (Saturday Night Live)

"@dlustv: Trump SNL Episode Generates Highest Ratings Since 2012: At the very least, Donald Trump is making Sat... http://bit.ly/1NDnKnI "

NOV 8, 2015 4:55 PM

.@NBCNews is bad but Saturday Night Live is the worst of NBC. Not funny, cast is terrible, always a complete hit job. Really bad television!

JAN 15, 2017 2:46 PM

Hamilton

The cast and producers of Hamilton, which I hear is highly overrated, should immediately apologize to Mike Pence for their terrible behavior

NOV 20, 2016 6:22 AM

Electoral College

Campaigning for votes under the Electoral College system is much more difficult, and different, than the popular vote.

DELETED AFTER 13 SECONDS AT 7:54 AM ON DEC 21, 2016

More "FAKE" News

(1/2).@FoxNews "Outgoing CIA Chief, John Brennan, blasts Pres-Elect Trump on Russia threat. Does not fully understand." Oh really, couldn't do...

JAN 15, 2017 4:16 PM

(2/2) much worse - just look at Syria (red line), Crimea, Ukraine and the build-up of Russian nukes. Not good! Was this the leaker of Fake News?

JAN 15, 2017 4:29 PM

If Russia, or some other entity, was hacking, why did the White House waite so long to act? Why did they only complain after Hillary lost?

DELETED AFTER 1 HOUR AT 9:59 AM ON DEC 15, 2016

The real story here is why are there so many illegal leaks coming out of Washington? Will these leaks be happening as I deal on N.Korea etc?

FEB 14, 2017 6:28 AM

Just leaving Florida. Big crowds of enthusiastic supporters lining the road that the FAKE NEWS media refuses to mention. Very dishonest!

FEB 12, 2017 2:19 PM

While on FAKE NEWS @CNN, Bernie Sanders was cut off for using the term fake news to describe the network. They said technical difficulties!

FEB 12, 2017 4:14 AM

The failing @ nytimes does major FAKE NEWS China story saying "Mr.Xi has not spoken to Mr. Trump since Nov.14." We spoke at length yesterday!

FEB 10, 2017 5:35 AM

Sticking It To "Haters and Losers"

I know Mark Cuban well. He backed me big-time but I wasn't interested in taking all of his calls.He's not smart enough to run for president!

FEB 12, 2017 5:23 AM

Ivanka Trump

My daughter Ivanka has been treated so unfairly by @Nordstrom. She is a great person -- always pushing me to do the right thing! Terrible!

FEB 8, 2017 7:51 AM

I am so proud of my daughter Ivanka. To be abused and treated so badly by the media, and to still hold her head so high, is truly wonderful!

FEB 11, 2017 3:00 PM

Failed Missions

(1/3) Sen. McCain should not be talking about the success or failure of a mission to the media. Only emboldens the enemy! He's been losing so....

FEB 9, 2017 5:26 AM

(2/3)...long he doesn't know how to win anymore, just look at the mess our country is in - bogged down in conflict all over the place. Our hero..

FEB 9, 2017 5:31 AM

(3/3) Ryan died on a winning mission (according to General Mattis), not a "failure." Time for the U.S. to get smart and start winning again!

FEB 9, 2017 5:52 AM

Sen.Richard Blumenthal, who never fought in Vietnam when he said for years he had (major lie),now misrepresents what Judge Gorsuch told him?

FEB 9, 2017 3:57 AM

Chris Cuomo, in his interview with Sen. Blumenthal, never asked him about his long-term lie about his brave "service" in Vietnam. FAKE NEWS!

FEB 9, 2017 5:19 AM

More

Big increase in traffic into our country from certain areas, while our people are far more vulnerable, as we wait for what should be EASY D!

FEB 8, 2017 9:41 AM

It is a disgrace that my full Cabinet is still not in place, the longest such delay in the history of our country. Obstruction by Democrats!

FEB 7, 2017 5:04 PM

If the U.S. does not win this case as it so obviously should, we can never have the security and safety to which we are entitled. Politics!

FEB 8, 2017 4:03 AM

I don't know Putin, have no deals in Russia, and the haters are going crazy - yet Obama can make a deal with Iran, #1 in terror, no problem!

FEB 7, 2017 4:11 AM

The failing @nytimes was forced to apologize to its subscribers for the poor reporting it did on my election win. Now they are worse!

FEB 6, 2017 6:33 PM

The failing @nytimes writes total fiction concerning me. They have gotten it wrong for two years, and now are making up stories & sources!

FEB 6, 2017 8:32 AM

I call my own shots, largely based on an accumulation of data, and everyone knows it. Some FAKE NEWS media, in order to marginalize, lies!

FEB 6, 2017 4:07 AM

Any negative polls are fake news, just like the CNN, ABC, NBC polls in the election. Sorry, people want border security and extreme vetting.

FEB 6, 2017 4:01 AM

Just cannot believe a judge would put our country in such peril. If something happens blame him and court system. People pouring in. Bad!

FEB 5, 2017 12:39 PM

I have instructed Homeland Security to check people coming into our country VERY CAREFULLY. The courts are making the job very difficult!

FEB 5, 2017 12:42 PM

The judge opens up our country to potential terrorists and others that do not have our best interests at heart. Bad people are very happy!

FEB 4, 2017 4:48 PM

The opinion of this so-called judge, which essentially takes law-enforcement away from our country, is ridiculous and will be overturned!

FEB 4, 2017 5:12 AM

We must keep "evil" out of our country!

FEB 3, 2017 3:08 PM

Professional anarchists, thugs and paid protesters are proving the point of the millions of people who voted to MAKE AMERICA GREAT AGAIN!

FEB 3, 2017 3:48 AM

Yes, Arnold Schwarzenegger did a really bad job as Governor of California and even worse on the Apprentice...but at least he tried hard!

FEB 3, 2017 3:24 AM

If U.C. Berkeley does not allow free speech and practices violence on innocent people with a different point of view - NO FEDERAL FUNDS?

FEB 2, 2017 3:13 AM

Everybody is arguing whether or not it is a BAN. Call it what you want, it is about keeping bad people (with bad intentions) out of country!

FEB 1, 2017 4:50 AM

When will the Democrats give us our Attorney General and rest of Cabinet! They should be ashamed of themselves! No wonder D.C. doesn't work!

JAN 31, 2017 3:27 AM

The Democrats are delaying my cabinet picks for purely political reasons. They have nothing going but to obstruct. Now have an Obama A.G.

JAN 30, 2017 4:45 PM

Only 109 people out of 325,000 were detained and held for questioning. Big problems at airports were caused by Delta computer outage,.....

JAN 30, 2017 4:16 AM

The joint statement of former presidential candidates John McCain & Lindsey Graham is wrong - they are sadly weak on immigration. The two...

JAN 29, 2017 1:45 PM

...Senators should focus their energies on ISIS, illegal immigration and border security instead of always looking to start World War III.

JAN 29, 2017 1:49 PM

Somebody with aptitude and conviction should buy the FAKE
NEWS and failing @nytimes and either run it correctly or let it fold
with dignity!

JAN 29, 2017 5:00 AM

Thr coverage about me in the @nytimes and the @washingtonpost
gas been so false and angry that the times actually apologized to
its.....

JAN 28, 2017 5:08 AM

...dwindling subscribers and readers. They got me wrong right from
the beginning and still have not changed course, and never will.
DISHONEST

JAN 28, 2017 5:16 AM

Ungrateful TRAITOR Chelsea Manning, who should never have
been released from prison, is now calling President Obama a weak
leader. Terrible!

JAN 26, 2017 3:04 AM

I will be asking for a major investigation into VOTER FRAUD,
including those registered to vote in two states, those who are illegal
and....

JAN 25, 2017 4:10 AM

even, those registered to vote who are dead (and many for a long
time). Depending on results, we will strengthen up voting procedures!

JAN 25, 2017 4:13 AM

If Chicago doesn't fix the horrible "carnage" going on, 228 shootings
in 2017 with 42 killings (up 24% from 2016), I will send in the
Feds!

JAN 24, 2017 6:25 PM

Congratulations to @FoxNews for being number one in inauguration ratings. They were many times higher than FAKE NEWS @CNN - public is smart!

JAN 24, 2017 6:16 PM

Watched protests yesterday but was under the impression that we just had an election! Why didn't these people vote? Celebs hurt cause badly.

JAN 22, 2017 4:47 AM

Had a great meeting at CIA Headquarters yesterday, packed house, paid great respect to Wall, long standing ovations, amazing people. WIN!

JAN 22, 2017 4:35 AM

January 20th 2017, will be remembered as the day the people became the rulers of this nation again.

JAN 20, 2017 9:53 AM

"It wasn't Donald Trump that divided this country, this country has been divided for a long time!" Stated today by Reverend Franklin Graham.

JAN 19, 2017 4:52 AM

Response to Allegations of Ties to Russia (After Resignation of Michael Flynn)

The fake news media is going crazy with their conspiracy theories and blind hatred. @MSNBC & @CNN are unwatchable. @foxandfriends is great!

FEB 15, 2017 3:40 AM

This Russian connection non-sense is merely an attempt to cover-up the many mistakes made in Hillary Clinton's losing campaign.

FEB 15, 2017 4:08 AM

Information is being illegally given to the failing @nytimes & @washingtonpost by the intelligence community (NSA and FBI?). Just like Russia

Feb 15, 2017 4:19 AM

Thank you to Eli Lake of The Bloomberg View - "The NSA & FBI... should not interfere in our politics...and is" Very serious situation for USA

Feb 15, 2017 4:28 AM

Crimea was TAKEN by Russia during the Obama Administration. Was Obama too soft on Russia?

Feb 15, 2017 4:42 AM

The real scandal here is that classified information is illegally given out by "intelligence" like candy. Very un-American!

Feb 15, 2017 5:13 AM

The Democrats had to come up with a story as to why they lost the election, and so badly (306), so they made up a story - RUSSIA. Fake news!

Feb 16, 2017 6:39 AM

FAKE NEWS media, which makes up stories and "sources," is far more effective than the discredited Democrats - but they are fading fast!

Feb 16, 2017 6:10 AM

The spotlight has finally been put on the low-life leakers! They will be caught!

Feb 16, 2017 4:02 AM

Leaking, and even illegal classified leaking, has been a big problem in Washington for years. Failing @nytimes (and others) must apologize!

Feb 16, 2017 3:58 AM

Stock market hits new high with longest winning streak in decades. Great level of confidence and optimism - even before tax plan rollout!

FEB 16, 2017 3:34 AM

Despite the long delays by the Democrats in finally approving Dr. Tom Price, the repeal and replacement of ObamaCare is moving fast!

FEB 17, 2017 2:13 AM

Thank you for all of the nice statements on the Press Conference yesterday. Rush Limbaugh said one of greatest ever. Fake media not happy!

FEB 17, 2017 3:43 AM

The FAKE NEWS media (failing @nytimes, @NBCNews, @ABC, @CBS, @CNN) is not my enemy, it is the enemy of the American People!

FEB 17, 2017 1:48 PM

"One of the most effective press conferences I've ever seen!" says Rush Limbaugh. Many agree. Yet FAKE MEDIA calls it differently! Dishonest

FEB 17, 2017 3:15 PM

Don't believe the main stream (fake news) media. The White House is running VERY WELL. I inherited a MESS and am in the process of fixing it.

FEB 18, 2017 5:31 AM

My statement as to what's happening in Sweden was in reference to a story that was broadcast on @FoxNews concerning immigrants & Sweden.

FEB 19, 2017 1:57 PM

The so-called angry crowds in home districts of some Republicans are actually, in numerous cases, planned out by liberal activists. Sad!

FEB 21, 2017 6:23 PM

White House Operations

Don't believe the main stream (fake news) media. The White House is running VERY WELL. I inherited a MESS and am in the process of fixing it.

FEB 18, 2017 8:31 AM

Will be having many meetings this weekend at The Southern White House. Big 5:00 P.M. speech in Melbourne, Florida. A lot to talk about!

FEB 18, 2017 8:51 AM

Bowling Green 2.0

My statement as to what's happening in Sweden was in reference to a story that was broadcast on @FoxNews concerning immigrants & Sweden.

FEB 19, 2017 4:57 PM

Give the public a break - The FAKE NEWS media is trying to say that large scale immigration in Sweden is working out just beautifully. NOT!

FEB 20, 2017 9:15 AM

'Americans overwhelmingly oppose sanctuary cities' https://t.co/s5QvsJWA6u

FEB 21, 2017 3:46 PM

Paid Protesters (Again)

The so-called angry crowds in home districts of some Republicans are actually, in numerous cases, planned out by liberal activists. Sad!

FEB 21, 2017 6:23 PM

Maybe the millions of people who voted to MAKE AMERICA GREAT AGAIN should have their own rally. It would be the biggest of them all!

FEB 25, 2017 7:25 AM

DNC Chair

One thing I will say about Rep. Keith Ellison, in his fight to lead the DNC, is that he was the one who predicted early that I would win!

FEB 22, 2017 7:20 AM

The race for DNC Chairman was, of course, totally "rigged." Bernie's guy, like Bernie himself, never had a chance. Clinton demanded Perez!

FEB 26, 2017 6:33 AM

More Fake News

FAKE NEWS media knowingly doesn't tell the truth. A great danger to our country. The failing @nytimes has become a joke. Likewise @CNN. Sad!

FEB 24, 2017 10:09 PM

The media has not reported that the National Debt in my first month went down by $12 billion vs a $200 billion increase in Obama first mo.

FEB 25, 2017 8:19 AM

Russia talk is FAKE NEWS put out by the Dems, and played up by the media, in order to mask the big election defeat and the illegal leaks!

FEB 26, 2017 1:16 PM

Does anybody really believe that a reporter, who nobody ever heard of, "went to his mailbox" and found my tax returns? @NBCNews FAKE NEWS!

MAR 15, 2017 5:55 AM

Just watched the totally biased and fake news reports of the so-called Russia story on NBC and ABC. Such dishonesty!

MAR 23, 2017 7:18 AM

Mainstream (FAKE) media refuses to state our long list of achievements, including 28 legislative signings, strong borders & great optimism!

APR 29, 2017 12:39 PM

The Fake News media is officially out of control. They will do or say anything in order to get attention - never been a time like this!

MAY 4, 2017 6:02 AM

Sorry folks, but if I would have relied on the Fake News of CNN, NBC, ABC, CBS, washpost or nytimes, I would have had ZERO chance winning WH

JUN 6, 2017 7:15 AM

JOBS! JOBS! JOBS!

Since November 8th, Election Day, the Stock Market has posted $3.2 trillion in GAINS and consumer confidence is at a 15 year high. Jobs!

MAR 2, 2017 6:00 AM

Buy American & hire American are the principles at the core of my agenda, which is: JOBS, JOBS, JOBS! Thank you @exxonmobil.

MAR 6, 2017 10:49 PM

Economic confidence is soaring as we unleash the power of private sector job creation and stand up for the American Workers. #AmericaFirst

APR 12, 2017 6:09 PM

One by one we are keeping our promises - on the border, on energy, on jobs, on regulations. Big changes are happening!

APR 12, 2017 6:10 PM

Jobs are returning, illegal immigration is plummeting, law, order and justice are being restored. We are truly making America great again!

APR 12, 2017 7:32 PM

Jeff Sessions

Jeff Sessions is an honest man. He did not say anything wrong. He could have stated his response more accurately, but it was clearly not....

MAR 2, 2017 9:22 PM

...intentional. This whole narrative is a way of saving face for Democrats losing an election that everyone thought they were supposed.....

MAR 2, 2017 9:27 PM

...to win. The Democrats are overplaying their hand. They lost the election, and now they have lost their grip on reality. The real story...

MAR 2, 2017 9:35 PM

...is all of the illegal leaks of classified and other information. It is a total "witch hunt!"

MAR 2, 2017 9:38 PM

Just out: The same Russian Ambassador that met Jeff Sessions visited the Obama White House 22 times, and 4 times last year alone.

MAR 4, 2017 6:42 AM

His Cabinet Still Isn't Full

It is so pathetic that the Dems have still not approved my full Cabinet.

MAR 3, 2017 7:19 AM

Demanding Investigations (On Twitter)

We should start an immediate investigation into @SenSchumer and his ties to Russia and Putin. A total hypocrite! https://t.co/Ik3yqjHzsA

MAR 3, 2017 12:54 PM

I hereby demand a second investigation, after Schumer, of Pelosi for her close ties to Russia, and lying about it. https://t.co/qCDljfF3wN

MAR 3, 2017 4:02 PM

Wire Tapping

Terrible! Just found out that Obama had my "wires tapped" in Trump Tower just before the victory. Nothing found. This is McCarthyism!

MAR 4, 2017 6:35 AM

Is it legal for a sitting President to be "wire tapping" a race for president prior to an election? Turned down by court earlier. A NEW LOW!

MAR 4, 2017 6:49 AM

I'd bet a good lawyer could make a great case out of the fact that President Obama was tapping my phones in October, just prior to Election!

MAR 4, 2017 6:52 AM

How low has President Obama gone to tapp my phones during the very sacred election process. This is Nixon/Watergate. Bad (or sick) guy!

MAR 4, 2017 7:02 AM

Is it true the DNC would not allow the FBI access to check server or other equipment after learning it was hacked? Can that be possible?

MAR 5, 2017 6:32 AM

When will Sleepy Eyes Chuck Todd and @NBCNews start talking about the Obama SURVEILLANCE SCANDAL and stop with the Fake Trump/Russia story?

APR 1, 2017 7:43 AM

The big story is the "unmasking and surveillance" of people that took place during the Obama Administration.

JUN 1, 2017 6:05 AM

Arnold

Arnold Schwarzenegger isn't voluntarily leaving the Apprentice, he was fired by his bad (pathetic) ratings, not by me. Sad end to great show

MAR 4, 2017 8:19 AM

Obama Sucks Tweets

122 vicious prisoners, released by the Obama Administration from Gitmo, have returned to the battlefield. Just another terrible decision!

MAR 7, 2017 7:04 AM

For eight years Russia "ran over" President Obama, got stronger and stronger, picked-off Crimea and added missiles. Weak! @foxandfriends

MAR 7, 2017 8:13 AM

Don't let the FAKE NEWS tell you that there is big infighting in the Trump Admin. We are getting along great, and getting major things done!

MAR 7, 2017 9:14 AM

The weak illegal immigration policies of the Obama Admin. allowed bad MS 13 gangs to form in cities across U.S. We are removing them fast!

APR 18, 2017 4:39 AM

Trumpcare

Don't worry, getting rid of state lines, which will promote competition, will be in phase 2 & 3 of healthcare rollout. @foxandfriends

MAR 7, 2017 8:41 AM

I feel sure that my friend @RandPaul will come along with the new and great health care program because he knows Obamacare is a disaster!

MAR 7, 2017 7:14 PM

Despite what you hear in the press, healthcare is coming along great. We are talking to many groups and it will end in a beautiful picture!

MAR 9, 2017 12:01 PM

We are making great progress with healthcare. ObamaCare is imploding and will only get worse. Republicans coming together to get job done!

MAR 11, 2017 9:39 AM

ObamaCare is imploding. It is a disaster and 2017 will be the worst year yet, by far! Republicans will come together and save the day.

MAR 13, 2017 8:11 AM

After seven horrible years of ObamaCare (skyrocketing premiums & deductibles, bad healthcare), this is finally your chance for a great plan!

MAR 24, 2017 7:14 AM

The Democrats will make a deal with me on healthcare as soon as ObamaCare folds - not long. Do not worry, we are in very good shape!

MAR 27, 2017 9:03 PM

You can't compare anything to ObamaCare because ObamaCare is dead. Dems want billions to go to Insurance Companies to bail out donors....New

APR 30, 2017 7:28 AM

...healthcare plan is on its way. Will have much lower premiums & deductibles while at the same time taking care of pre-existing conditions!

APR 30, 2017 7:32 AM

I am very supportive of the Senate #HealthcareBill. Look forward to making it really special! Remember, ObamaCare is dead.

JUN 22, 2017 3:40 PM

If Republican Senators are unable to pass what they are working on now, they should immediately REPEAL, and then REPLACE at a later date!

JUN 30, 2017 3:37 AM

Women's Rights

A conspicuously different tone than was struck toward women in earlier tweets…

I have tremendous respect for women and the many roles they serve that are vital to the fabric of our society and our economy.

MAR 8, 2017 6:12 AM

On International Women's Day, join me in honoring the critical role of women here in America & around the world.

MAR 8, 2017 6:13 AM

Celebrity Reactions

Can you imagine what the outcry would be if @SnoopDogg, failing career and all, had aimed and fired the gun at President Obama? Jail time!

MAR 15, 2017 6:02 AM

Fox News Plugs

RT @foxandfriends: FOX NEWS ALERT: Jihadis using religious visa to enter US, experts warn (via @FoxFriendsFirst) https://t.co/pwXeR9OMQC

MAR 17, 2017 7:34 AM

Just heard Fake News CNN is doing polls again despite the fact that their election polls were a WAY OFF disaster. Much higher ratings at Fox

MAR 20, 2017 7:35 AM

Watch @foxandfriends now on Podesta and Russia!

MAR 28, 2017 6:16 AM

Why doesn't Fake News talk about Podesta ties to Russia as covered by @FoxNews or money from Russia to Clinton - sale of Uranium?

MAR 28, 2017 5:41 PM

Such amazing reporting on unmasking and the crooked scheme against us by @foxandfriends. "Spied on before nomination." The real story.

APR 3, 2017 5:15 AM

Wow, @FoxNews just reporting big news. Source: "Official behind unmasking is high up. Known Intel official is responsible. Some unmasked....

APR 1, 2017 11:50 AM

..not associated with Russia. Trump team spied on before he was nominated." If this is true, does not get much bigger. Would be sad for U.S.

APR 1, 2017 12:02 PM

RT @foxandfriends: Former President Obama's $400K Wall Street speech stuns liberal base; Sen. Warren saying she "was troubled by that"

APR 28, 2017 7:12 AM

Congratulations to @foxandfriends on its unbelievable ratings hike.

MAY 4, 2017 6:07 AM

RT @foxandfriends: President Trump to sign an executive order on religious liberty today, the National Day of Prayer

MAY 4, 2017 6:09 AM

.@FoxNews from multiple sources: "There was electronic surveillance of Trump, and people close to Trump. This is unprecedented." @FBI

APR 3, 2017 7:51 AM

"The first 90 days of my presidency has exposed the total failure of the last eight years of foreign policy!" So true. @foxandfriends

APR 17, 2017 7:07 AM

.@foxandfriends Dems are taking forever to approve my people, including Ambassadors. They are nothing but OBSTRUCTION-ISTS! Want approvals.

JUN 5, 2017 8:35 AM

RT @foxandfriends: FOX NEWS ALERT: ISIS claims responsibility for hostage siege in Melbourne, Australia that killed 1 person and injured 3...

JUN 6, 2017 5:43 AM

Foreign Relations

Despite what you have heard from the FAKE NEWS, I had a GREAT meeting with German Chancellor Angela Merkel. Nevertheless, Germany owes.....

MAR 18, 2017 8:15 AM

...vast sums of money to NATO & the United States must be paid more for the powerful, and very expensive, defense it provides to Germany!

MAR 18, 2017 8:23 AM

The meeting next week with China will be a very difficult one in that we can no longer have massive trade deficits...

MAR 30, 2017 5:16 PM

...and job losses. American companies must be prepared to look at other alternatives.

MAR 30, 2017 5:16 PM

Leaks to the Press

The real story that Congress, the FBI and all others should be looking into is the leaking of Classified information. Must find leaker now!

MAR 20, 2017 6:02 AM

What about all of the contact with the Clinton campaign and the Russians? Also, is it true that the DNC would not let the FBI in to look?

MAR 20, 2017 8:14 AM

The real story turns out to be SURVEILLANCE and LEAKING! Find the leakers.

APR 2, 2017 8:34 AM

Trump Rallies (He Still Holds Them)

Thanks you for all of the Trump Rallies today. Amazing support. We will all MAKE AMERICA GREAT AGAIN!

MAR 25, 2017 5:37 PM

Looking forward to RALLY in the Great State of Pennsylvania tonight at 7:30. Big crowd, big energy!

APR 29, 2017 10:35 AM

Big excitement last night in the Great State of Pennsylvania! Fantastic crowd and people. MAKE AMERICA GREAT AGAIN!

APR 30, 2017 7:05 AM

Getting ready to leave for Cincinnati, in the GREAT STATE of OHIO, to meet with ObamaCare victims and talk Healthcare & also Infrastructure!

JUN 7, 2017 7:17 AM

Freedom Caucus

The irony is that the Freedom Caucus, which is very pro-life and against Planned Parenthood, allows P.P. to continue if they stop this plan!

MAR 24, 2017 7:23 AM

Democrats are smiling in D.C. that the Freedom Caucus, with the help of Club For Growth and Heritage, have saved Planned Parenthood & Ocare!

MAR 26, 2017 7:21 AM

The Republican House Freedom Caucus was able to snatch defeat from the jaws of victory. After so many bad years they were ready for a win!

MAR 27, 2017 8:41 PM

The Freedom Caucus will hurt the entire Republican agenda if they don't get on the team, & fast. We must fight them, & Dems, in 2018!

MAR 30, 2017 8:07 AM

Investigations

Why isn't the House Intelligence Committee looking into the Bill & Hillary deal that allowed big Uranium to go to Russia, Russian speech....

MAR 27, 2017 8:26 PM

...money to Bill, the Hillary Russian "reset," praise of Russia by Hillary, or Podesta Russian Company. Trump Russia story is a hoax. #MAGA!

MAR 27, 2017 8:35 PM

Was the brother of John Podesta paid big money to get the sanctions on Russia lifted? Did Hillary know?

APR 3, 2017 6:16 AM

Did Hillary Clinton ever apologize for receiving the answers to the debate? Just asking!

APR 3, 2017 6:21 AM

Media Coverage

Remember when the failing @nytimes apologized to its subscribers, right after the election, because their coverage was so wrong. Now worse!

MAR 29, 2017 7:01 AM

If the people of our great country could only see how viciously and inaccurately my administration is covered by certain media!

MAR 29, 2017 7:21 AM

The failing @nytimes has disgraced the media world. Gotten me wrong for two solid years. Change libel laws? https://t.co/QIqLgvYLLi

MAR 30, 2017 9:27 AM

It is the same Fake News Media that said there is "no path to victory for Trump" that is now pushing the phony Russia story. A total scam!

APR 1, 2017 8:02 AM

The failing @nytimes finally gets it - "In places where no insurance company offers plans, there will be no way for ObamaCare customers to..

APR 1, 2017 10:59 AM

...use subsidies to buy health plans." In other words, Ocare is dead. Good things will happen, however, either with Republicans or Dems.

APR 1, 2017 11:06 AM

Anybody (especially Fake News media) who thinks that Repeal & Replace of ObamaCare is dead does not know the love and strength in R Party!

APR 2, 2017 7:56 AM

Fake News is at an all time high. Where is their apology to me for all of the incorrect stories???

JUN 13, 2017 5:48 AM

Mike Flynn

Mike Flynn should ask for immunity in that this is a witch hunt (excuse for big election loss), by media & Dems, of historic proportion!

MAR 31, 2017 6:04 AM

General Flynn was given the highest security clearance by the Obama Administration - but the Fake News seldom likes talking about that.

MAY 8, 2017 6:57 AM

Syrian Missile Strike

The reason you don't generally hit runways is that they are easy and inexpensive to quickly fix (fill in and top)!

APR 8, 2017 2:00 PM

More on China

I explained to the President of China that a trade deal with the U.S. will be far better for them if they solve the North Korean problem!

APR 11, 2017 6:59 AM

North Korea is looking for trouble. If China decides to help, that would be great. If not, we will solve the problem without them! U.S.A.

APR 11, 2017 7:03 AM

I have great confidence that China will properly deal with North Korea. If they are unable to do so, the U.S., with its allies, will! U.S.A.

APR 13, 2017 8:08 AM

Things will work out fine between the U.S.A. and Russia. At the right time everyone will come to their senses & there will be lasting peace!

APR 13, 2017 8:16 AM

Why would I call China a currency manipulator when they are working with us on the North Korean problem? We will see what happens!

APR 16, 2017 7:18 AM

China is very much the economic lifeline to North Korea so, while nothing is easy, if they want to solve the North Korean problem, they will

APR 21, 2017 8:04 AM

North Korea disrespected the wishes of China & its highly respected President when it launched, though unsuccessfully, a missile today. Bad!

APR 28, 2017 6:26 PM

North Korea has shown great disrespect for their neighbor, China, by shooting off yet another ballistic missile...but China is trying hard!

MAY 29, 2017 7:18 AM

Low Bar

TRUMP APPROVAL HITS 50% https://t.co/vjZkGTyQb9

APR 17, 2017 5:38 PM

Tax March

I did what was an almost an impossible thing to do for a Republican-easily won the Electoral College! Now Tax Returns are brought up again?

APR 16, 2017 8:07 AM

Someone should look into who paid for the small organized rallies yesterday. The election is over!

APR 16, 2017 8:13 AM

Democratic Candidates

The recent Kansas election (Congress) was a really big media event, until the Republicans won. Now they play the same game with Georgia-BAD!

APR 16, 2017 7:45 PM

The Fake Media (not Real Media) has gotten even worse since the election. Every story is badly slanted. We have to hold them to the truth!

Apr 17, 2017 7:17 AM

The super Liberal Democrat in the Georgia Congressioal race tomorrow wants to protect criminals, allow illegal immigration and raise taxes!

Apr 17, 2017 8:31 AM

With eleven Republican candidates running in Georgia (on Tuesday) for Congress, a runoff will be a win. Vote "R" for lower taxes & safety!

Apr 17, 2017 9:18 PM

Democrat Jon Ossoff would be a disaster in Congress. VERY weak on crime and illegal immigration, bad for jobs and wants higher taxes. Say NO

Apr 18, 2017 5:38 AM

Republicans must get out today and VOTE in Georgia 6. Force runoff and easy win! Dem Ossoff will raise your taxes-very bad on crime & 2nd A.

Apr 18, 2017 5:46 AM

Just learned that Jon @Ossoff, who is running for Congress in Georgia, doesn't even live in the district. Republicans, get out and vote!

Apr 18, 2017 3:38 PM

Despite major outside money, FAKE media support and eleven Republican candidates, BIG "R" win with runoff in Georgia. Glad to be of help!

Apr 18, 2017 11:09 PM

Democrat Jon Ossoff, who wants to raise your taxes to the highest level and is weak on crime and security, doesn't even live in district.

Jun 20, 2017 2:49 AM

Paris Attack

Another terrorist attack in Paris. The people of France will not take much more of this. Will have a big effect on presidential election!

APR 21, 2017 5:32 AM

First 100 Days

No matter how much I accomplish during the ridiculous standard of the first 100 days, & it has been a lot (including S.C.), media will kill!

APR 21, 2017 5:50 AM

Environmentalism

Today on Earth Day, we celebrate our beautiful forests, lakes and land. We stand committed to preserving the natural beauty of our nation.

APR 22, 2017 2:01 PM

The Wall

(1/2) I am reading that the great border WALL will cost more than the government originally thought, but I have not gotten involved in the. . . .

FEB 11, 2017 5:18 AM

(2/2)...design or negotiations yet. When I do, just like with the F-35 FighterJet or the Air Force One Program, price will come WAY DOWN!

FEB 11, 2017 5:24 AM

The Democrats don't want money from budget going to border wall despite the fact that it will stop drugs and very bad MS 13 gang members.

APR 23, 2017 10:42 AM

Eventually, but at a later date so we can get started early, Mexico will be paying, in some form, for the badly needed border wall.

APR 23, 2017 10:44 AM

The Wall is a very important tool in stopping drugs from pouring into our country and poisoning our youth (and many others)! If

APR 24, 2017 7:28 AM

....the wall is not built, which it will be, the drug situation will NEVER be fixed the way it should be! #BuildTheWall

APR 24, 2017 10:31 AM

Don't let the fake media tell you that I have changed my position on the WALL. It will get built and help stop drugs, human trafficking etc.

APR 25, 2017 7:36 AM

The Election

New polls out today are very good considering that much of the media is FAKE and almost always negative. Would still beat Hillary in .....

APR 23, 2017 2:48 PM

...popular vote. ABC News/Washington Post Poll (wrong big on election) said almost all stand by their vote on me & 53% said strong leader.

APR 23, 2017 2:55 PM

The two fake news polls released yesterday, ABC & NBC, while containing some very positive info, were totally wrong in General E. Watch!

APR 24, 2017 7:15 AM

Crooked Hillary Clinton now blames everybody but herself, refuses to say she was a terrible candidate. Hits Facebook & even Dems & DNC.

MAY 31, 2017 7:40 PM

O, Canada!

Canada has made business for our dairy farmers in Wisconsin and other border states very difficult. We will not stand for this. Watch!

APR 25, 2017 7:30 AM

Trade Deficits

The U.S. recorded its slowest economic growth in five years (2016). GDP up only 1.6%. Trade deficits hurt the economy very badly.

Apr 26, 2017 5:51 AM

Federal Budget

Democrats are trying to bail out insurance companies from disastrous #ObamaCare, and Puerto Rico with your tax dollars. Sad!

Apr 26, 2017 6:06 PM

The Democrats want to shut government if we don't bail out Puerto Rico and give billions to their insurance companies for OCare failure. NO!

Apr 27, 2017 6:30 AM

I want to help our miners while the Democrats are blocking their healthcare.

Apr 27, 2017 9:37 AM

I promise to rebuild our military and secure our border. Democrats want to shut down the government. Politics!

Apr 27, 2017 9:37 AM

Democrats jeopardizing the safety of our troops to bail out their donors from insurance companies. It is time to put #AmericaFirst⊠⊠

Apr 27, 2017 9:38 AM

Democrats used to support border security — now they want illegals to pour through our borders.

Apr 27, 2017 9:39 AM

As families prepare for summer vacations in our National Parks - Democrats threaten to close them and shut down the government. Terrible!

Apr 27, 2017 9:39 AM

The reason for the plan negotiated between the Republicans and Democrats is that we need 60 votes in the Senate which are not there! We....

MAY 2, 2017 8:01 AM

either elect more Republican Senators in 2018 or change the rules now to 51%. Our country needs a good "shutdown" in September to fix mess!

MAY 2, 2017 8:07 AM

NAFTA

I received calls from the President of Mexico and the Prime Minister of Canada asking to renegotiate NAFTA rather than terminate. I agreed..

APR 27, 2017 6:12 AM

...subject to the fact that if we do not reach a fair deal for all, we will then terminate NAFTA. Relationships are good-deal very possible!

APR 27, 2017 6:21 AM

I will be interviewed on @FaceTheNation this morning at 10:00 A.M. Have a great day!

APR 30, 2017 6:33 AM

Andrew Jackson

President Andrew Jackson, who died 16 years before the Civil War started, saw it coming and was angry. Would never have let it happen!

MAY 1, 2017 7:55 PM

James Comey

FBI Director Comey was the best thing that ever happened to Hillary Clinton in that he gave her a free pass for many bad deeds! The phony...

MAY 2, 2017 9:51 PM

...Trump/Russia story was an excuse used by the Democrats as justification for losing the election. Perhaps Trump just ran a great campaign?

MAY 2, 2017 10:06 PM

Cryin' Chuck Schumer stated recently, "I do not have confidence in him (James Comey) any longer." Then acts so indignant. #draintheswamp

MAY 9, 2017 9:42 PM

The Democrats have said some of the worst things about James Comey, including the fact that he should be fired, but now they play so sad!

MAY 10, 2017 6:10 AM

James Comey will be replaced by someone who will do a far better job, bringing back the spirit and prestige of the FBI.

MAY 10, 2017 6:19 AM

Comey lost the confidence of almost everyone in Washington, Republican and Democrat alike. When things calm down, they will be thanking me!

MAY 10, 2017 6:27 AM

Watching Senator Richard Blumenthal speak of Comey is a joke. "Richie" devised one of the greatest military frauds in U.S. history. For....(1/3)

MAY 10, 2017 7:24 AM

years, as a pol in Connecticut, Blumenthal would talk of his great bravery and conquests in Vietnam - except he was never there. When.... (2/3)

MAY 10, 2017 7:30 AM

caught, he cried like a baby and begged for forgiveness...and now he is judge & jury. He should be the one who is investigated for his acts. (3/3)

MAY 10, 2017 7:39 AM

James Comey better hope that there are no "tapes" of our conversations before he starts leaking to the press!

MAY 12, 2017 7:26 AM

When James Clapper himself, and virtually everyone else with knowledge of the witch hunt, says there is no collusion, when does it end?

MAY 12, 2017 7:54 AM

The Roger Stone report on @CNN is false - Fake News. Have not spoken to Roger in a long time - had nothing to do with my decision.

MAY 10, 2017 7:57 AM

I have been asking Director Comey & others, from the beginning of my administration, to find the LEAKERS in the intelligence community.....

MAY 16, 2017 7:10 AM

Despite so many false statements and lies, total and complete vindication...and WOW, Comey is a leaker!

JUN 9, 2017 3:10 AM

With all of the recently reported electronic surveillance, intercepts, unmasking and illegal leaking of information, I have no idea...

JUN 22, 2017 9:54 AM

...whether there are "tapes" or recordings of my conversations with James Comey, but I did not make, and do not have, any such recordings.

JUN 22, 2017 9:55 AM

Susan Rice

Susan Rice, the former National Security Advisor to President Obama, is refusing to testify before a Senate Subcommittee next week on.....

MAY 4, 2017 5:40 AM

...allegations of unmasking Trump transition officials. Not good!

MAY 4, 2017 5:49 AM

More on Trumpcare (Passed in the House)

The Democrats, without a leader, have become the party of obstruction. They are only interested in themselves and not in what's best for U.S.

APR 30, 2017 7:09 AM

I am watching the Democrats trying to defend the "you can keep you doctor, you can keep your plan & premiums will go down" ObamaCare lie."

MAY 4, 2017 12:43 PM

Insurance companies are fleeing ObamaCare - it is dead. Our healthcare plan will lower premiums & deductibles - and be great healthcare!

MAY 4, 2017 12:56 PM

If victorious, Republicans will be having a big press conference at the beautiful Rose Garden of the White House immediately after vote!

MAY 4, 2017 1:07 PM

Big win in the House - very exciting! But when everything comes together with the inclusion of Phase 2, we will have truly great healthcare!

MAY 5, 2017 7:52 AM

2 million more people just dropped out of ObamaCare. It is in a death spiral. Obstructionist Democrats gave up, have no answer = resist!

JUN 13, 2017 6:56 AM

Meanwhile, Melania Lives in Trump Tower

Rather than causing a big disruption in N.Y.C., I will be working out of my home in Bedminster, N.J. this weekend. Also saves country money!

MAY 5, 2017 8:02 AM

The reason I am staying in Bedminster, N. J., a beautiful community, is that staying in NYC is much more expensive and disruptive. Meetings!

MAY 6, 2017 5:39 PM

Fake News and Obamacare

Of course the Australians have better healthcare than we do --everybody does. ObamaCare is dead! But our healthcare will soon be great.

MAY 5, 2017 2:13 PM

Wow,the Fake News media did everything in its power to make the Republican Healthcare victory look as bad as possible.Far better than Ocare!

MAY 5, 2017 6:22 PM

Why is it that the Fake News rarely reports Ocare is on its last legs and that insurance companies are fleeing for their lives? It's dead!

MAY 5, 2017 6:29 PM

Some of the Fake News Media likes to say that I am not totally engaged in healthcare. Wrong, I know the subject well & want victory for U.S.

JUN 28, 2017 3:58 AM

Trump/Russia Connection

When will the Fake Media ask about the Dems dealings with Russia & why the DNC wouldn't allow the FBI to check their server or investigate?

MAY 7, 2017 6:15 AM

Ask Sally Yates, under oath, if she knows how classified information got into the newspapers soon after she explained it to W.H. Counsel.

MAY 8, 2017 9:43 AM

Director Clapper reiterated what everybody, including the fake media already knows- there is "no evidence" of collusion w/ Russia and Trump.

MAY 8, 2017 5:41 PM

Sally Yates made the fake media extremely unhappy today --- she said nothing but old news!

MAY 8, 2017 5:43 PM

The Russia-Trump collusion story is a total hoax, when will this taxpayer funded charade end?

MAY 8, 2017 5:46 PM

Biggest story today between Clapper & Yates is on surveillance. Why doesn't the media report on this? #FakeNews!

MAY 8, 2017 5:50 PM

Russia must be laughing up their sleeves watching as the U.S. tears itself apart over a Democrat EXCUSE for losing the election.

MAY 11, 2017 3:34 PM

Again, the story that there was collusion between the Russians & Trump campaign was fabricated by Dems as an excuse for losing the election.

MAY 12, 2017 6:51 AM

The Fake Media is working overtime today!

MAY 12, 2017 6:53 AM

By the way, if Russia was working so hard on the 2016 Election, it all took place during the Obama Admin. Why didn't they stop them?

JUN 22, 2017 6:22 AM

Cancelling Press Briefings

As a very active President with lots of things happening, it is not possible for my surrogates to stand at podium with perfect accuracy!....

MAY 12, 2017 6:59 AM

...Maybe the best thing to do would be to cancel all future "press briefings" and hand out written responses for the sake of accuracy???

MAY 12, 2017 7:07 AM

Sharing Info with Russia

As President I wanted to share with Russia (at an openly scheduled W.H. meeting) which I have the absolute right to do, facts pertaining.... (1/2)

MAY 16, 2017 6:03 AM

...to terrorism and airline flight safety. Humanitarian reasons, plus I want Russia to greatly step up their fight against ISIS & terrorism. (2/2)

MAY 16, 2017 6:13 AM

Real News?

China just agreed that the U.S. will be allowed to sell beef, and other major products, into China once again. This is REAL news!

MAY 12, 2017 8:20 AM

This is the single greatest witch hunt of a politician in American history!

MAY 18, 2017 6:52 AM

With all of the illegal acts that took place in the Clinton campaign &
Obama Administration, there was never a special counsel appointed!

MAY 18, 2017 9:07 AM

Trump's First Foreign Trip

Getting ready for my big foreign trip. Will be strongly protecting
American interests - that's what I like to do!

MAY 19, 2017 9:24 AM

Many NATO countries have agreed to step up payments consider-
ably, as they should. Money is beginning to pour in- NATO will be
much stronger.

MAY 27, 2017 5:03 AM

Just arrived in Italy after having a very successful NATO meeting
in Brussels. Told other nations they must pay more, not fair to U.S.

MAY 28, 2017 6:57 AM

Fake News and Russia Probe

It is my opinion that many of the leaks coming out of the White
House are fabricated lies made up by the #FakeNews media.

MAY 28, 2017 7:33 AM

Whenever you see the words 'sources say' in the fake news media,
and they don't mention names.... (1/2)

MAY 28, 2017 7:34 AM

....it is very possible that those sources don't exsist but are made up
by fake news writers. #FakeNews is the enemy! (2/2)

MAY 28, 2017 7:35 AM

Does anyone notice how the Montana Congressional race was such
a big deal to Dems & Fake News until the Republican won? V was
poorly covered (repeated at 7:45 the same day)

MAY 28, 2017 7:40 AM

British Prime Minister May was very angry that the info the U.K. gave to U.S. about Manchester was leaked. Gave me full details!

MAY 28, 2017 9:43 AM

The Fake News Media works hard at disparaging & demeaning my use of social media because they don't want America to hear the real story!

MAY 28, 2017 7:20 PM

So now it is reported that the Democrats, who have excoriated Carter Page about Russia, don't want him to testify. He blows away their.... (1/2)

MAY 31, 2017 5:37 AM

...case against him & now wants to clear his name by showing "the false or misleading testimony by James Comey, John Brennan..." Witch Hunt! (2/2)

MAY 31, 2017 5:45 AM

They made up a phony collusion with the Russians story, found zero proof, so now they go for obstruction of justice on the phony story. Nice

JUN 15, 2017 3:55 AM

Why is that Hillary Clintons family and Dems dealings with Russia are not looked at, but my non-dealings are?

JUN 15, 2017 12:43 PM

Crooked H destroyed phones w/ hammer, 'bleached' emails, & had husband meet w/AG days before she was cleared- & they talk about obstruction?

JUN 15, 2017 12:56 PM

After 7 months of investigations & committee hearings about my "collusion with the Russians," nobody has been able to show any proof. Sad!

JUN 16, 2017 4:53 AM

The Fake News Media hates when I use what has turned out to be my very powerful Social Media - over 100 million people! I can go around them

JUN 16, 2017 5:23 AM

Kathy Griffin Photo
In which she was holding a fake decapitated Trump head...

Kathy Griffin should be ashamed of herself. My children, especially my 11 year old son, Barron, are having a hard time with this. Sick!

MAY 31, 2017 6:14 AM

Covfefe
Despite the constant negative press covfefe

MAY 30, 2017 11:06 PM

Who can figure out the true meaning of "covfefe" ??? Enjoy!

MAY 31, 2017 05:09 AM

The Travel Ban and London
We need to be smart, vigilant and tough. We need the courts to give us back our rights. We need the Travel Ban as an extra level of safety!

JUN 3, 2017 6:17 PM

At least 7 dead and 48 wounded in terror attack and Mayor of London says there is "no reason to be alarmed!"

JUN 4, 2017 6:31 AM

Do you notice we are not having a gun debate right now? That's because they used knives and a truck!

JUN 4, 2017 6:43 AM

People, the lawyers and the courts can call it whatever they want, but I am calling it what we need and what it is, a TRAVEL BAN!

JUN 5, 2017 5:25 AM

The Justice Dept. should have stayed with the original Travel Ban, not the watered down, politically correct version they submitted to S.C.

JUN 5, 2017 5:29 AM

The Justice Dept. should ask for an expedited hearing of the watered down Travel Ban before the Supreme Court - & seek much tougher version!

JUN 5, 2017 5:37 AM

In any event we are EXTREME VETTING people coming into the U.S. in order to help keep our country safe. The courts are slow and political!

JUN 5, 2017 5:44 AM

Pathetic excuse by London Mayor Sadiq Khan who had to think fast on his "no reason to be alarmed" statement. MSM is working hard to sell it!

JUN 5, 2017 8:49 AM

That's right, we need a TRAVEL BAN for certain DANGEROUS countries, not some politically correct term that won't help us protect our people!

JUN 5, 2017 8:20 PM

On Deleting Twitter

The FAKE MSM is working so hard trying to get me not to use Social Media. They hate that I can get the honest and unfiltered message out.

JUN 6, 2017 6:58 AM

Qatar

During my recent trip to the Middle East I stated that there can no longer be funding of Radical Ideology. Leaders pointed to Qatar - look!

JUN 6, 2017 7:06 AM

So good to see the Saudi Arabia visit with the King and 50 countries already paying off. They said they would take a hard line on funding...(1/2)

JUN 6, 2017 8:36 AM

...extremism, and all reference was pointing to Qatar. Perhaps this will be the beginning of the end to the horror of terrorism! (2/2)

JUN 6, 2017 8:44 AM

The "Witch Hunt"

You are witnessing the single greatest WITCH HUNT in American political history - led by some very bad and conflicted people! #MAGA

JUN 15, 2017 4:57 AM

Despite the phony Witch Hunt going on in America, the economic & jobs numbers are great. Regulations way down, jobs and enthusiasm way up!

JUN 16, 2017 5:54 AM

I am being investigated for firing the FBI Director by the man who told me to fire the FBI Director! Witch Hunt

JUN 16, 2017 6:07 AM

The MAKE AMERICA GREAT AGAIN agenda is doing very well despite the distraction of the Witch Hunt. Many new jobs, high business enthusiasm,..

JUN 18, 2017 3:38 AM

The Breaking Point?

I heard poorly rated @Morning_Joe speaks badly of me (don't watch anymore). Then how come low I.Q. Crazy Mika, along with Psycho Joe, came.

JUN 29, 2017 5:52 AM

...to Mar-a-Lago 3 nights in a row around New Year's Eve, and insisted on joining me. She was bleeding badly from a face-lift. I said no!

JUN 29, 2017 5:58 AM

Endnotes

1   Fromm, Erich, *The Heart of Man* (New York: American Mental Health Foundation, 1964) 63.

2   Ibid.

3   Ibid.

4   Kernberg, Otto. "Factors in the psychoanalytic treatment of narcissistic personalities," J. Am. Psychoanal. Assoc. 18:51-85, 1970.

5   Goode, Erica. "The world: Stalin to Saddam: So much for the madman theory," *New York Times*, 5/4/03.

6   Ibid.

7   Pollock, G. H. "Process and affect," *International Journal of Psycho-Analysis*, 59, pp. 255–276, 1978.

8   Radio Interview with Michael Savage on *The Savage Nation* on February 16, 2016.

9   Phone interview with *Fox News* on May 3, 2016.

10 Holan, Angie and Linda Qui. "2015 lie of the year: the campaign misstatements of Donald Trump," *Politifact*, 12/21/15; Cheney, Kyle, et al. "Donald Trump's week of misrepresentations, exaggerations, and half-truths," *Politico*, 9/25/16.

11 Gass, Nick. "New York AG: Trump U 'really a fraud from beginning to end,'" *Politico*, 9/25/16.

12 Q&A at the Family Leadership Summit in Ames, Iowa, July 18, 2015.

13 Ibid.

14 Diamond, Jeremy. "Donald Trump on protester: 'I'd like to punch him in the face'," *CNN*, February 23, 2016.

15 DelReal, Jose A. "Trump mocks sexual assault accuser: 'She would not be my first choice.'" *The Washington Post*, October 14, 2016.

16 Solotaroff, Paul. "Trump Seriously: On the Trail With the GOP's Tough Guy," *Rolling Stone*, September 9, 2015.

17 Carissimo, Justin. "Megyn Kelly to Donald Trump: 'You've called women you don't like fat pigs, slobs – and disgusting animals'," *Independent*, August 7, 2015.

18 Higgins, Andrew. "Trump Embraces 'Enemy of the People,' a Phrase With a Fraught History," *The New York Times*, February 26, 2017.

19 Schulberg, Jessica. "Russian Disinformation Works Because Donald Trump 'Parrots The Same Lines,' Cyber Expert Testifies," *The Huffington Post*, March 30, 2017.

20 Ibid.

21 Ibid.

22 Parker, Ashley and David E. Sanger. "Donald Trump Calls on Russia to Find Hillary Clinton's Missing Emails," *The New York Times*, July 27, 2016.

23 Reisner, Steven. "Stop saying Donald Trump is mentally ill," *Slate*, 3/15/17.

24 Television interview on *The Last Word with Lawrence O'Donnell, MSNBC*, 2/21/2017, http://www.msnbc.com/transcripts/the-last-word/2017-02-21.

25 Gartner, John. "What is Trump's Psychological Problem?" *The Huffington Post*, 06/09/2016.

26 Fromm, *The Heart of Man*.

27 Tansey, PhD, Michael J. "Part X. Trump and the Codes: Why 'Crazy Like a Fox' vs. 'Crazy Like a Crazy' Really Matters." *The Huffington Post*, 03/19/2017.

28 Ibid.

29 Gartner, PhD, John. "Donald Trump and Bill Clinton Have the Same Secret Weapon," *New Republic*, August 25, 2015.

30 Trump, Donald with Meredith McIver. *Trump: Think Like a Billionaire: Everything You Need to Know About Success, Real Estate, and Life*. New York: Random House Publishing, 2004.

31 Ibid.

32 Ibid.

33 Ibid.

34 Kruse, Michael. "1988: The Year Donald Lost His Mind," *Politico Magazine*, March 11, 2016.

35 Ibid.

36 Brooks, David. "Trump's Enablers Will Finally Have to Take a Stand," *The New York Times*, August 5, 2016.

37 Fromm, *The Heart of Man*.

38 Ibid.